A
WORLD
WITHOUT
WAR

A

WORLD

WITHOUT

WAR

'Abdu'l-Bahá and the
Discourse for Global Peace

Hoda Mahmoudi and Janet A. Khan

BAHÁ'Í
PUBLISHING

WILMETTE, ILLINOIS

Bahá'í Publishing
401 Greenleaf Avenue, Wilmette, Illinois 60091

23   22   21   20   4   3   2   1

Library of Congress Cataloging-in-Publication Data
Names: Mahmoudi, Hoda, author. | Khan, Janet A. (Janet Adrienne), 1940–
    author.
Title: A world without war : 'Abdu'l-Bahá and the discourse for global
    peace / Hoda Mahmoudi and Janet Khan.
Description: Wilmette, Illinois : Bahá'í Publishing, 2020. | Includes
    bibliographical references and index.
Identifiers: LCCN 2020020760 (print) | LCCN 2020020761 (ebook) | ISBN
    9781618511645 (trade paperback) | ISBN 9781618511669 (kindle edition)
Subjects: LCSH: Peace—Religious aspects—Bahai Faith. | 'Abdu'l-Bahá,
    1844–1921. | Bahá'u'lláh, 1817-1892. | Bahai Faith—Doctrines.
Classification: LCC BP388.P43 M34 2020 (print) | LCC BP388.P43 (ebook) |
    DDC 297.9/317273—dc23
LC record available at https://lccn.loc.gov/2020020760
LC ebook record available at https://lccn.loc.gov/2020020761

Cover design by Carlos Esparza
Book design by Patrick Falso

Contents

Acknowledgments

The authors are grateful to many people who have made the publication of this book possible. We wish to thank Dr. Kate Seaman, Mr. Alawi Masud, Mr. Malik Wilson, Dr. Nushafarin Fathi, Dr. Homa Mahmoudi, Mr. Hamid Mozaffari, and Mr. Lloyd Griffith.

We specially wish to thank Ms. Guity Javid, the granddaughter of Aḥmad Yazdání. Mr. Aḥmad Yazdání and Hand of the Cause Ibn-i-Aṣdaq were the two Persian Bahá'ís appointed by 'Abdu'l-Bahá to travel to The Netherlands in 1920, to deliver 'Abdu'l-Bahá's message on peace to the Executive Committee of the Central Organization for a Durable Peace at The Hague.

Our gratitude also goes out to the Research Department at the Bahá'í World Center, Haifa, Israel, and to the editorial staff at the United States Bahá'í Publishing Trust, Wilmette, IL.

Preface

June 2020 marks one hundred years since the two historic Tablets of 'Abdu'l-Bahá* were delivered to the Central Organization for a Durable Peace at The Hague. The Tablets,** combined with His public talks that were presented during His travels in the West between 1911 and 1913, offer comprehensive insights about Bahá'u'lláh's panoramic vision for the attainment of universal peace. World peace is a primary objective of the religion founded by Bahá'u'lláh in mid-nineteenth century Iran. The Tablets to The Hague and the public talks of His son 'Abdu'l-Bahá serve as a model for participation in the public discourses of society. They also provide an example of His profound involvement in the life of society and His acute understanding of social reality. Furthermore, in His Tablets and talks, He outlines the process involved in developing the climate conducive to the construction of a new social order and the emergence of the institutions associated with Bahá'u'lláh's World Order.

In this volume, the historical circumstances that shaped nineteenth-century peace movements and the catastrophic impact of the First World War are examined. During the time these significant events were unfolding,

---

* Son of Bahá'u'lláh, Founder of the Bahá'í Faith.
** Letters.

Preface

'Abdu'l-Bahá was actively engaged in promoting a clear understanding of the Bahá'í perspective on peace. Far more than simply focusing His discourse on the means to end wars, 'Abdu'l-Bahá offered the holistic, all-inclusive vision for global peace—the oneness of humanity—outlined in the Writings of Bahá'u'lláh. The historical context is important to having a thorough appreciation of the contribution 'Abdu'l-Bahá made to the discourses for global peace that were taking place before and immediately after World War I.

This book illustrates 'Abdu'l-Bahá's strategic language and energetic approach toward communicating His Father's vision. It highlights the priority He accorded the current issues of His day and the manner in which He correlated them with the Bahá'í teachings. His engagement with intellectuals and leaders of thought on the subject of the implementation of peace provided an outstanding model for humanity during the early years of the twentieth century, and His example has continuing relevance for the state of the world and the discourse on peace in the twenty-first century.

1 / Enlarging the Framework for Peace

In recent years, the centenary of the end of the First World War has resulted in much thoughtful reflection on the causes of war and its destructive impact on the peoples and nations of the world, and on the international order. A hundred years later, with the benefit of hindsight, historians and commentators continue to ponder the meaning of the war and the nature of the peace settlement that emerged from the conference convened in Paris in 1919.[1] Military historian Hew Strachan observes that such anniversary celebrations provide an opportunity to take a fresh look at historical evidence, with all its diversity and complexity, and to reach new understandings and altered perspectives on the phenomena of war and peace.[2]

As a contribution to the process of re-envisaging the idea of peace, this book offers a Bahá'í perspective on the concept of peace. The book, *A World Without War*, examines, through the prism of the involvement of 'Abdu'l-Bahá—the son of Bahá'u'lláh, founder of the Bahá'í Faith—in the discourses of nineteenth and early twentieth-century society, the critical period leading up to World War I. It illustrates 'Abdu'l-Bahá's lifelong commitment to the establishment of universal peace and His ability to take the Writings of Bahá'u'lláh and apply them to contemporary social issues.

The analysis revolves around three interrelated topics pertaining to the example of 'Abdu'l-Bahá's life and His active promotion, both within the Bahá'í community and the world at large, of values conducive to the emergence of

1

a culture of peace. Particular consideration is given to 'Abdu'l-Bahá's peace activities—primarily in the West—including His talks, contact with leaders of thought, activists, and groups that promoted peace, and His participation at the 1912 Lake Mohonk* conference. We also examine the significant role played by 'Abdu'l-Bahá's Tablets of the Divine Plan in ensuring the promotion of peace throughout the five continents of the globe, and we describe in detail an episode that took place a century ago in the aftermath of World War I, in which 'Abdu'l-Bahá addressed two Tablets outlining the Bahá'í vision for an integrated approach to world peace to the Executive Committee of the Central Organization for a Durable Peace at The Hague. The Central Organization for a Durable Peace, set up in 1915, was an international group of influential peace activists and legal experts committed to promoting widespread discussion about the prerequisites for a sustainable peace. The Organization ended its work at the end of WWI. The League of Nations was officially established in 1920.

As a framework for exploring 'Abdu'l-Bahá's contribution to an enlarged understanding of peace, it is necessary to examine the approach to peace outlined in the literature of the Bahá'í Faith, describe the stages envisaged in the progressive unfoldment of peace, and to consider the state of the world prior to World War I and in its immediate aftermath, and outline some of the efforts made to achieve peace during the same period. Against this backdrop, the contemporary relevance of the work of 'Abdu'l-Bahá can be more fully appreciated, especially as it relates to the unfinished business of world peace, which has resulted from the persistent obstacles standing in its way. It is interesting to note that in engaging in the discourses of society, 'Abdu'l-Bahá called attention to principles and ideas in the Writings of the Bahá'í Faith that pertain to peace. He offered these perspectives as a contribution to enhanced understanding and to the transformation of society at the level of thought.[3]

---

* In upstate New York.

Enlarging the Framework for Peace

The objective of the Bahá'í Faith as laid out in the teachings of its founder, Bahá'u'lláh, is the attainment of universal peace. Although all world religions anticipate a time when world peace will be realized, the conditions have not yet been suitable for the attainment of a holistic, all-inclusive, global peace. Bahá'u'lláh's conception of peace is comprehensive and far-reaching. The framework for its attainment is based on His set of ideas, principles, and laws intended to change and restructure relationships among the nation-states as well as to transform institutions and social norms.[4]

Chapter 2 places the Bahá'í Faith in a historical context and describes principles necessary to achieve an integrated and holistic approach to peace. It explores the paradigmatic importance of recognizing the oneness of the human family as a prerequisite to peace; examines some of the principles that are key to the promotion of peace; and describes the Bahá'í administrative structures that, as they continue to evolve, are critical to promoting the well-being of humankind.

Bahá'u'lláh stresses the importance of understanding the state of the world and the forces that are impinging on the life of the individual and society. "Every age," He states, "hath its own problem, and every soul its particular aspiration." It therefore follows, that "The remedy the world needeth in its present-day afflictions can never be the same as that which a subsequent age may require." He advises humankind: "Be anxiously concerned with the needs of the age ye live in, and center your deliberations on its exigencies and requirements."[5] As a framework within which to gain a deeper appreciation of 'Abdu'l-Bahá's astute observation of world affairs and His unique contribution to the promotion of peace, chapter 3 describes some of the forces for social and cultural change that were sweeping across the globe in the years leading up to World War I—forces that were competing for attention and influence, reorienting worldviews, challenging traditional customs and values, and impacting the lives of peoples throughout the world. This chapter also briefly reviews the primary factors leading to the outbreak of the First World War.

Chapter 4 examines the involvement of peace organizations and civil society in activities promoting peace in the years leading up to and immediately after the outbreak of World War I. We briefly describe earlier attempts to create a durable peace, including several significant peace gatherings that took place in The Hague, and we examine in detail the work and program of the Central Organization for a Durable Peace at The Hague.

Chapters 5 and 6 are devoted to an analysis of the three interrelated topics mentioned above pertaining to the example of 'Abdu'l-Bahá's life and His promotion of values conducive to the emergence of a culture of peace. Chapter 5 examines His services in the West and the continuing importance of the Tablets of the Divine Plan to the achievement of peace. Written between 1916 and 1917, during the darkest period of the First World War, these remarkable letters offered an alternative vision of the world, laid out strategies and guiding principles for achieving a peaceful world, and assigned certain responsibilities for spreading the values of peace throughout the globe.

Chapter 6 examines the circumstances surrounding the revelation by 'Abdu'l-Bahá of Tablets addressed to the Executive Committee of the Central Organization for a Durable Peace at The Hague and His appointment of a delegation consisting of two Persian Bahá'ís, Ibn-i-Aṣdaq and Aḥmad Yazdání, to travel to The Netherlands to deliver the Tablets and to serve as His representatives in meetings with the Organization. As a context for understanding the involvement of the Persian believers, we briefly describe the situation in Iran during World War I, and the two representatives' initial contact with the Central Organization. We describe the meetings of the delegation with the Organization, outline the contents of the Tablets, and review the response of the Central Organization to the Tablets.

The historical significance of the episode described above goes far beyond the actual encounters that took place between 'Abdu'l-Bahá's delegation and the Executive Committee at The Hague. Its enduring importance is linked to the contents of the letters that 'Abdu'l-Bahá wrote to the Executive Committee. Written a century ago, 'Abdu'l-Bahá's letters describe the Bahá'í perspec-

4

tive on comprehensive universal peace. He outlines essential ideas and concepts that provide the means by which the establishment of universal peace is made possible. For ease of reference, newly revised English translations of the letters sent to the Executive Committee are included in Appendix 2.

Chapter 7 begins by outlining the unfoldment of attempts to achieve peace at the end of World War I. It then discusses the enduring contribution of the contents of the Tablets to The Hague Organization to the attainment of peace in contemporary times and it reflects on the importance 'Abdu'l-Bahá accorded to His communication with the Central Organization, a group that in its heyday was committed to the promotion of widespread discourse on universal peace.

The final chapter, chapter 8, returns to a consideration of the Bahá'í perspective on the processes by which peace will emerge. It briefly outlines the unfoldment of various attempts by world leaders and peace organizations to achieve peace since the end of the First World War, reflects upon the unfinished business of peace, and assesses progress toward implementation of "an age of peace" characterized by "a collective state of being, manifesting unity."[6]

2 / The Bahá'í Faith and Peace: Principles of an Integrated, Holistic Peace

The Bahá'í Faith presents to the world a message of hope, of love, and practical reconstruction. Written in the nineteenth century, the divinely inspired teachings of Bahá'u'lláh are centered around the theme of the oneness of the human family and the unity of nations. They provide the direction and spiritual impetus to lead humanity to the new age of maturity, unity, and peace. Although all world religions anticipated a time when peace would be realized, the conditions were not yet suitable for the attainment of a universal peace—a holistic, all-inclusive global peace.

Bahá'u'lláh's conception of peace is comprehensive and far-reaching. It envisages not merely a peace that rules out armed conflict, but an age of peace characterized by "a collective state of being, manifesting unity."[1] The framework for its attainment is based on His set of ideas, principles, and laws intended to change and restructure relationships among the nation-states, institutions, and social norms.

The principal aim of the Bahá'í Faith is to foster the development of a spirit of unity that eliminates the social, ideological, cultural, and nationalistic barriers that have divided the human family. Its future-oriented teachings outline a pathway for constructing a new social order capable of meeting the demands and complexities of a rapidly changing world. The Bahá'í Faith offers a prescription for a way of living that enriches the individual socially,

7

intellectually, and spiritually. It achieves this end through commitment to universal education, through its uncompromising stand against all forms of prejudice and indoctrination, its firm and unyielding adherence to the principle of the equality of women, and its support of the principle that religion and science should be regarded as harmonious and complementary approaches to the pursuit of truth. At the heart of Bahá'u'lláh's teachings for such a profound transformation in human relationships is a strong moral or spiritual framework upon which the attainment of peace can be realized.

In addition to encouraging processes to reorient individual values and behavior, the principle of the oneness of humankind underpinning Bahá'u'lláh's vision of peace calls for a significant reconstruction of the present social order, including the interrelationships between the peoples of the world as well as the nation-states. It is envisaged that the achievement of global peace will eventually necessitate monumental structural changes in the international order. The means and details toward this goal are developed in the written works of Bahá'u'lláh and those of His chosen successors. The Bahá'í Writings unfold a vision for the establishment of world peace that will evolve gradually and traverse through different stages over a lengthy span of time. The process is organic, with setbacks and breakthroughs, yet always progressing toward developing greater levels of coordination and coherence among the evolving elements of an emergent global world order.

In this chapter, we review some of the basic Bahá'í concepts concerning the role of religion in the world, discuss principles vital to sustaining universal peace, and examine the multifaceted approach to peace outlined in the teachings of the Bahá'í Faith, the youngest of the monotheistic world religions. An overview of the Bahá'í teachings reveals a coherent strategy, as well as a holistic vision for peace that is inclusive of the entire human family.

Religion and the Historical Process

From a Bahá'í perspective, the course of history is, in large part, shaped by the intermittent intervention of the Divine Will in the historical process. Religion is, therefore, regarded as playing a critical role in society and the ongoing development of civilization. At the heart of Bahá'í belief is the concept of progressive revelation, which involves the coming of divine Educators, or Manifestations of God, at periodic intervals in various parts of the world over the span of thousands of years. Each of these Manifestations of God, Who are the Founders of the world's great religious systems, brings teachings appropriate to the needs of the age in which They appear. Their teachings provide the vision and values for the advance of civilization and propel humanity forward toward a promised time of world unity, human rights, and peace. Their seminal Writings and creative impulses, when translated into constructive action, unlock individual potential and stimulate social development.

The Bahá'í Faith was inaugurated in 1844 by the declaration of Mírzá 'Alí-Muḥammad (1819–1850), known as the Báb (Gate), that He was the bearer of a message from God, and that He was the Herald and Forerunner of a second Prophetic figure, Bahá'u'lláh, Whose coming was imminent and Whose mission would usher in an era of righteousness and peace. The dawn of the religion coincided with a period of millennial expectation, and its progressive teachings generated a high degree of interest and ferment among the population, initially in the Middle East and subsequently throughout the world.

The teachings of the new religion were perceived by the authorities in the Middle East as both a challenge to their power and to the established social and ecclesiastical order. The organized forces of church and state immediately launched a severe persecution against the Báb, precipitating His exile, imprisonment, and finally His execution by firing squad in Tabríz, Iran. Their concerted efforts were, likewise, directed toward the extermination of the nascent community. Indeed, the early history of the religion is drenched with the blood of thousands of its adherents, with the thirst for vengeance unquenched by the martyrdom of the Báb in 1850.

Mírzá Ḥusayn-'Alí (1817–1892), a Persian nobleman titled Bahá'u'lláh, Whose advent was foretold by the Báb, and to Whom the Báb's followers turned naturally for leadership after His martyrdom, was also assailed by the repressive forces of fanaticism. He was imprisoned for a period in an underground dungeon in Tehran in 1852 and upon His release was exiled to Baghdad along with the members of His immediate family and a number of His followers. Bahá'u'lláh's declaration of His prophetic mission in 1863 brought the full force of the civil and ecclesiastical opposition upon Him and His followers. He remained a prisoner and an exile for the rest of His life and was transferred successively to the Ottoman cities of Constantinople (Istanbul) and Adrianople (Edirne). Finally, He was exiled and incarcerated for a period of over twenty-four years in the notorious prison-city of 'Akká and its environs, on the Mediterranean coast, where He passed away in 1892. His remains were interred at Bahjí, on the outskirts of 'Akká.

The Bahá'í Faith is a religion of change and regards all human beings as having the true purpose of participating in an ever-advancing civilization. It aims to create unity between the diverse elements of humankind. Its teachings include principles that are directed to all aspects of human thought and conduct and that promote individual and social development. Central to Bahá'í belief is the view that "religious truth is not absolute but relative, that Divine Revelation is a continuous and progressive process, that all the great religions of the world are divine in origin, that their basic principles are in complete harmony, that their aims and purposes are one and the same, that their teachings are but facets of one truth, that their functions are complementary, that they differ only in the non-essential aspects of their doctrines, and that their missions represent successive stages in the spiritual evolution of human society."[2]

Bahá'u'lláh explains that all religions emanate from a single and common origin—God, and that every religion conveys spiritual and social knowledge and principles relevant to the age in which the religion is revealed. From time to time, humanity receives spiritual guidance through one of God's appointed Prophet-Founders Who instruct the people with new laws and spiritual teachings based on the requirements of a continually changing social order.

The Bahá'í Faith and Peace: Principles of an Integrated, Holistic Peace

From its inception in the nineteenth century, the Bahá'í Faith was introduced to humanity as a global religion; a religion that addresses the peoples of
both the West and the East—the entire global community.[3] In Bahá'u'lláh's
written works, a set of new ideas, principles, and institutional arrangements
are provided as the means toward the establishment of unity, justice, and
peace between the peoples and nations of the world. His Writings, taken as
a whole, present a blueprint of a complex, process-oriented approach toward
the formation of peace.

The concept of the progressive unfoldment of vision and capacity and the
process of social evolution are interconnected. For example, employing the
analogy of the stages of an individual life—infancy, childhood, adolescence,
and maturity—the Bahá'í teachings explain that humanity is approaching
its stage of maturity; maturity implies commitment, wisdom, responsibility,
humility, and gratitude: "Viewed through Bahá'u'lláh's eyes, the history of
tribes, peoples, and nations has effectively reached its conclusion. What we
are witnessing is the beginning of the history of humankind, the history of a
human race conscious of its own oneness. To this turning point in the course
of civilization, [Bahá'u'lláh's] Writings bring a redefinition of the nature and
processes of civilization and a reordering of its priorities. Their aim is to call
us back to spiritual awareness and responsibility."[4]

Every Manifestation or Prophet of God carries out a distinct mission with
teachings that are relevant to the particular time in which He unveils His
message. With the appearance of each Prophet, a spiritual renewal takes
shape with new ideas, timely concepts, and principles that gradually over
an extended period of time, stimulate a new vision and action in relation to
improved human relationships and society building. Spiritual education and
moral teachings derived from religion propel humanity to higher stages of
consciousness, to the further development of human capacity and specializa-
tion in service to society building and improving the human condition. Thus,
spiritual education and vision brought forth by each of the world's religions
stimulate human knowledge, instill wisdom, expand understanding, promote

greater creativity, stimulate progress, and build civilization. By this means, Bahá'u'lláh explains, "every man will advance and develop until he . . . can manifest all the potential forces with which his inmost true self hath been endowed,"[5] and will carry forward "an ever-advancing civilization."[6]

Religion serves as the stimulus, the motivation for change and progress through spiritual values that have the potential to shape customs, practices, culture, relations, institutions, and social structures. Spiritual teachings are intended to advance human cognition and broaden understanding about the purpose of both spiritual and material existence as the means to construct a better world.

An Integrated and Holistic Peace

The Bahá'í Faith had its origins in Iran in the middle of the nineteenth century. Its Founder, Bahá'u'lláh wrote extensively about the topic of peace, the obstacles that continue to impede its realization, and the arduous but inevitable process involved in its eventual attainment.

As noted above, the core principles of the Bahá'í Faith are the oneness of God and His religions, and the oneness of humankind. Bahá'u'lláh explains that all religions derive from a single, unknowable essence—God. These spiritual principles have fundamental practical implications for social evolution and peace. For example, the Bahá'í conception of the oneness of religion implies that the institution of religion, regardless of the name of its Founder and His specific teachings, emanates from God. Bahá'u'lláh refers to the process of the evolution of religion in human history as "progressive Revelation."[7] He explains that throughout history, a succession of religions has appeared under different names and "entrusted with a Message, and charged to act in a manner that would best meet the requirements of the age in which He [the Prophet-Founder] appeared."[8] The variations observed between the Founders and teachings of the major religions are "attributed to the varying receptivity of an ever-changing world."[9] Expounding on the features of progressive revelation or the evolution of religion in history, Bahá'u'lláh writes,

"I testify before God that each one of these Manifestations hath been sent down through the operation of the Divine Will and Purpose, that each hath been the bearer of a specific Message, that each hath been entrusted with a divinely revealed Book and been commissioned to unravel the mysteries of a mighty Tablet. The measure of the Revelation with which every one of them hath been identified had been definitely foreordained."[10]

In this manner, God, through His Messengers imparts knowledge to humanity about spiritual concepts and timely principles that enable people to gain new knowledge, insight, and discernment about social reality both individually and collectively. Bahá'u'lláh explains progressive revelation or the evolving role of religion in history in the following words: "This is the changeless Faith of God, eternal in the past, eternal in the future."[11] The purpose of religion, Bahá'u'lláh writes, "is to establish unity and concord amongst the peoples of the world."[12] He cautions humanity not to make it "the cause of dissension and strife."[13] His teachings also warn that, should religion become the cause of contention and animosity, its absence is preferable.[14] He also makes explicit that, "Religious fanaticism and hatred are a world-devouring fire, whose violence none can quench."[15]

"God's purpose in sending His Prophets unto men," according to Bahá'u'lláh, "is twofold. The first is to liberate the children of men from the darkness of ignorance, and guide them to the light of true understanding. The second is to ensure the peace and tranquility of mankind, and provide all means by which they can be established."[16]

Every religion conveys spiritual and social knowledge and principles relevant to the age in which the religion is revealed. In this fashion, religion is an evolving, ever-changing institution, a dynamic force that imparts spiritual and social teachings that address the challenges and possibilities presented by the age in which it appears. Bahá'u'lláh claimed that His Revelation was the latest but not final chapter in the ever-evolving religion of God.

Another critical principle of the Bahá'í Faith related to the establishment of world peace is the oneness of humankind. The concept of humanity as a single unified global family is linked to the establishment of global peace. The principle of the oneness of humankind also ties directly to the elimination of all forms of prejudice and the development of world-mindedness, and is fundamental to the process of constructing a world order whose interconnected systems of governance, economy, other social institutions, and cultures plausibly support and sustain the rapidly ever-changing global community.

The oneness of humankind—the experience of one common humanity—involves far more than bringing about kinship and fellowship among the peoples of the world. Rather, it is primarily concerned with the nature of the relationships and agreements that exist between the leaders of the nations and states. The depth and scale of changes that are required in order to support a fully interconnected and interdependent single humanity, as envisaged by Bahá'u'lláh, is developed in the Bahá'í Writings. Elaborating on this theme, Shoghi Effendi (1897–1957), the appointed successor of 'Abdu'l-Bahá, states: "[The oneness of humankind] does not constitute merely the enunciation of an ideal, but stands inseparably associated with an institution adequate to embody its truth, demonstrate its validity, and perpetuate its influence. It implies an organic change in the structure of present-day society, a change such as the world has not yet experienced. It constitutes a challenge, at once bold and universal, to outworn shibboleths of national creeds."[17]

Bahá'u'lláh assigned responsibility to the kings and religious leaders of the world to explore every means in their power to resolve the dangerous problems of humanity. They are entrusted with the authority to safeguard and ensure the security and tranquility of the people over whom they rule. In a series of letters and Writings, written in the late 1860s and 1870s, He called upon them to gather together and unite in their role as national leaders to resolve their differences, treat their citizens justly, provide them with opportunities, and foster human progress, prosperity, peace, and happiness. Among the leaders He addressed were Queen Victoria, Napoleon III, Czar Alexander II, King of Prussia and German Emperor William I, Francis Joseph of the Austro-Hungarian monarchy, Pope Pius IX, the Sultan of the

Ottoman Empire, the Qájár Shah of Iran, and rulers in America. Bahá'u'lláh urged the leaders, "Compose your differences and reduce your armaments, that the burden of your expenditures may be lightened, and that your minds and hearts may be tranquilized. Heal the dissensions that divide you, and ye will no longer be in need of any armaments except what the protection of your cities and territories demandeth."[18]

In these historic letters, Bahá'u'lláh called attention to the role of the kings and leaders to establishing solidarity and harmony among the nations. Recognizing their function as "the greatest means for insuring the tranquility of the nations"[19] and as "the chief instrument[s] for the protection of all mankind,"[20] Bahá'u'lláh reminded the rulers about their responsibilities to the people over whom they rule. He warned them about the unjust financial burden they place on their subjects, cautioned them about their duty in relation to the plight of the poor, and called upon them to act in taking measures to defend the well-being of the poor. "God hath committed into your hands the reins of the government of the people," Bahá'u'lláh wrote, "that ye may rule with justice over them, safeguard the rights of the downtrodden, and punish the wrongdoers."[21]

With respect to the relationships between the nations, Bahá'u'lláh directed the leaders of the world to achieve unity among themselves "for thereby will the tempest of discord be stilled amongst you, and your peoples find rest."[22] Indeed, He established the attainment of unity as a prerequisite to peace. "The well-being of mankind, its peace and security," Bahá'u'lláh wrote, "are unattainable unless and until its unity is firmly established."[23]

Bahá'u'lláh elucidated the prominent role and authority assumed by the leaders of the world in preventing wars and securing peace. He defined collective security and outlined the conditions within which the leaders must act to avert war:

The time must come when the imperative necessity for the holding of a vast, an all-embracing assemblage of men will be universally realized.

The rulers and kings of the earth must needs attend it, and, participating in its deliberations, must consider such ways and means as will lay the foundations of the world's Great Peace amongst men. Such a peace demandeth that the Great Powers should resolve, for the sake of the tranquility of the peoples of the earth, to be fully reconciled among themselves. Should any king take up arms against another, all should unitedly arise and prevent him. If this be done, the nations of the world will no longer require any armaments, except for the purpose of preserving the security of their realms and of maintaining internal order within their territories. This will ensure the peace and composure of every people, government and nation.[24]

And, further emphasizing the importance of collective security to the resolution of conflict and as an alternative to war, He states: "Should anyone among you [the sovereigns] take up arms against another, rise ye all against him, for this is naught but manifest justice."[25] The primary purpose of the application of the principle of collective security is to bring a swift end to conflict and war.

There are numerous moral and spiritual principles enunciated in Bahá'u'lláh's letters to the leaders of the world. Suffice it to say that His purpose in writing to the leaders of empires, nations, and to the religious leaders was not only to remind them of their unique responsibility in leading and governing their affairs, but also to offer them the opportunity of becoming instruments in transforming the international order by advancing the well-being of their people, enhancing the relationships between the nations, and harmonizing relationships among the followers of the world's religions.

In contemporary times, the process of globalization has profoundly impacted relationships between the nations. There is a growing trend towards interdependence and worldwide interconnectedness that challenges the traditional doctrine of independent national sovereignty that has, for generations, tended to characterize notions of international governance. For example, in the economic sector, developments in worldwide trade, finance, and production have given rise to the emergence of global markets in a single capitalist economy. Production and marketing are organized by multinational corporations on a global basis. Whether countries receive credit and under what terms is determined by global financial markets. Another example of worldwide interconnectedness involves the military in relation to the global arms trade, transnational terrorism, and proliferation of weapons of mass destruction.

Global migration patterns have also created major global issues throughout the world. Clear borders between nations are important. However, as emphasized by Shoghi Effendi in 1936, "Nation-building has come to an end. The anarchy inherent in state sovereignty is moving towards a climax. A world, growing to maturity, must abandon this fetish, recognize the oneness and wholeness of human relationships, and establish once for all the machinery that can best incarnate this fundamental principle of its life."[26] Scholars in international relations call attention to a notable structural change that took place in the 1990s in institutional arrangements within the international order. The change involved "a shift from a more or less cooperative system of states based on Westphalian sovereignty and intergovernmentalism to a global governance system."[27] What took place in the global governance system that differed from the Westphalian model, was its "double constituency" where both states and societal actors now have rights and obligations.[28] Global governance and its practices in world politics are set apart from ideas about the international system based on Westphalian sovereignty. Instead of Westphalian anarchy, the global governance system rests on three normative principles that contstrain the principle of sovereignty. It points to the assumption that there is a global common good, which is more than the sum of individual state interest. Otherwise, it would not make sense to justify global governance in those terms. Second, the global governance system refers to an inscription of individual rights and societal entitlements as parts of the normative structure of world politics. The right of justification—if autonomy is reduced by international institutions—applies not only to states, but also to individuals. At the same time, member states must fulfill minimal criteria internally before they are considered as recognized members. Lastly, in order to substantiate these underlying norms, the concept of global governance includes the possibility of international authority undermining the Westphalian idea of states as exclusive holders of final authority.[29]

Global governance as described, indicates that there are domains of authority beyond the nation-state, "without necessarily requiring a legal-doctrinal acceptance of the supremacy of international law."[30] Although the current global governance system upholds certain standards or normativity, as a whole, the system is not just or peaceful. Relationships between nation-states in their present form, are politically unequal and largely dictated by the more powerful states. The imbalance of power among the nations has negative implications for the less powerful states, which are vulnerable to acts of aggression on the part of the more powerful ones.

The problems afflicting the world are not resolvable without a serious level of collective action on the part of the nations toward addressing the ongoing fragmentation, conflicts, and chaos that bring harm upon the masses of innocent people. Take, for example, the challenges posed by global inequalities, economic crises and injustice, climate change, food and water security, pandemics, cybersecurity, or the exorbitant expenses and resources committed to the worldwide spread of militarization and weapons of war. These and many other grand-scale social problems confronting the world and its peoples are completely insoluble by a single nation-state. The leaders of nations have the capacity and power to consider pragmatic and an all-inclusive collective action to reorganize the international community in order to remove the obstacles to the disorder in the world. They have the authority to draw up, between their nation-states, treaties that offer strong provisions to realistically address the ever-demanding needs of an evolving complicated interlinked world order. A new paradigm for global governance is called for.

A New Paradigm

The Bahá'í teachings concerning the oneness of humankind provides an alternative context within which to explore elements of a new paradigm in global governance. The practice and attainment of this principle is a critical prerequisite to the organization and maintenance of peace. It calls for the development of relationships among the nation-states of the world that are capable of coordinating the different elements of a complex and evolving global political and social order. The concept may be likened to the system of political organization under federalism where separate states are united under the umbrella of one political system. Under federal systems, a written constitution provides the terms for both shared and divided power between the government and the states that constitute the federal union. The coherent political system of federated states is decentralized and does not permit one state to be more autonomous than another.

Many scholars and activists question the nation-state's capability to solve global problems.[31] A system of governance that realistically supports the needs and requirements of a common humanity is the basis of Bahá'u'lláh's principle of the oneness of humankind. The world has entered a phase of fundamental and accelerated change—a level and quality of change that it has not experienced before in its history. What Bahá'u'lláh brings attention to is the need for humanity to face the challenges by "subordinating all lesser loyalties and limiting identities to their oneness as citizens of a single plane-tary homeland."[32] At the same time, the Bahá'í principle of unity in diversity highlights another crucial aspect in relation to guarding against oppression and suppression of any part of what forms the human family—culture, lan-guage, religion, ethnic origin, and the like. Subordinating one's lesser loyalties and identities for the greater good is intended in no way to threaten the existing foundations of society. The Bahá'í Writings expand on the implications of the concept of unity in diversity:

> It [The Bahá'í Faith] can conflict with no legitimate allegiances, nor can it undermine essential loyalties. Its purpose is neither to stifle the flame of a sane and intelligent patriotism in men's hearts, nor to abolish the system of national autonomy so essential if the evils of excessive centralization are to be avoided. It does not ignore, nor does it attempt to suppress, the diversity of ethnical origins, of climate, of history, of language and tradition, of thought and habit, that differentiate the peoples and nations of the world. It calls for a wider loyalty, for a larger aspiration than any that has animated the human race. It insists upon the subordination of national impulses and interests to the imperative claims of a unified world. It repudiates excessive centralization on one hand, and disclaims all attempts at uniformity on the other.[33]

Unique to Bahá'u'lláh's Revelation is His inauguration of a pattern—a blueprint for constructing a new world order—of a decentralized global community, with institutions of governance whose fundamental goal is to create a civilization capable of supporting the oneness of humankind and to advance the social order toward world peace. Along these lines, it is imperative to understand Bahá'u'lláh's vision about the purpose of His religion: "My object is none other than the betterment of the world and the tranquility of its peoples. The well-being of mankind, its peace and security, are unattainable unless and until its unity is firmly established."[34]

Drawing attention to the flawed, outdated, fragmented, and broken present social order, Bahá'u'lláh states, "Soon will the present-day order be rolled up, and a new one spread out in its stead."[35] Observing that "The world's equilibrium hath been upset through the vibrating influence of this most great, this new World Order,"[36] He envisages the emergence of a "System" capable of meeting the urgent requirements posed by an ever-changing interconnected new "World Order" which His revelation will bring into being.

Shoghi Effendi identifies the Bahá'í Administrative Order with the "System" referred to by Bahá'u'lláh. Consisting of institutions ordained by Bahá'u'lláh, the Administrative Order is responsible for promoting the spiritual and material well-being, happiness, and peace of not only the Bahá'í community but of humanity. These institutions are the "nucleus" and "pattern" of Bahá'u'lláh's evolving World Order, or the future Bahá'í "world Commonwealth." Shoghi Effendi confirms that the Administrative Order "will, as its component parts, its organic institutions, begin to function with efficiency and vigor, assert its claim and demonstrate its capacity to be regarded not only as the nucleus but the very pattern of the New World Order destined to embrace in the fullness of time the whole of mankind."[37] As they gain knowledge and experience in applying spiritual principles to the social and economic development of their communities, these institutions form the structure that supports a new emerging social order with growing capacity to match the ongoing challenges and changes taking shape in a highly interconnected world.

Integral to the Bahá'í administrative structure are its provisions to avoid the enduring schisms that have grievously diminished the strength and cohesion of many religions as a consequence of disagreements over authority and organization after the passing of the Founder. These provisions are contained in the Covenant of Bahá'u'lláh, which sets out explicitly in writing the arrangements for authority and organization after His passing. The Covenant designates the appointed successor and provides for the establishment of Bahá'í administrative institutions to guide the affairs of the religion. Bahá'u'lláh in His Will appointed His eldest son, 'Abdu'l-Bahá as the Interpreter of His Writings and head of the Faith. 'Abdu'l-Bahá, in His Will and Testament, identified His Twin Successors: His eldest grandson, Shoghi Effendi, as appointed Guardian of the Faith, and the elected body of the Universal House of Justice ordained by Bahá'u'lláh.

To bring into being the Bahá'í administrative structure, specified in the Covenant of Bahá'u'lláh, Shoghi Effendi gave special attention to establishing and consolidating the administrative institutions throughout the world and to elucidating both the principles and methods of operation of this evolving administrative system. By discharging his functions, which included acting as the authorized interpreter of the Faith, Shoghi Effendi successfully completed his mission to expand and protect the fledgling Faith by the time of his own passing in 1957.

The Bahá'í Faith has no priesthood and is free from the privileges, prerogatives, and rituals that are generally associated with ecclesiastical structures. The Bahá'í Administrative Order has two arms. It consists on the one hand of democratically elected bodies operating at the local, national and international levels of society. The internationally elected body, the Universal House of Justice, was ordained by Bahá'u'lláh, and is the head of the Bahá'í Faith. It was first elected in 1963. These institutions are endowed with the authority to administer the affairs of their Bahá'í community in their respective jurisdictions through the exercise of legislative, judicial, and executive powers. Moreover, they are to serve as a channel through which the spiritual essence of the Bahá'í teachings are extended out to the larger society in creating relationships that unite people in actions that serve to advance and sustain society toward its collective maturity.

The second arm of the Administrative Order is composed of individuals appointed to act in an advisory capacity to the elected bodies at all levels and to individuals, to both protect and propagate the Faith. They offer counsel, foster adherence to the spiritual values of the religion, have primary roles in the educative processes of the Bahá'í community, and call attention to those measures required to protect the Bahá'í Faith from inadvertent or malicious corruption of its teachings. These individuals are designated as Counselors and Auxiliary Board members, and, along with their assistants, are organized into five boards of Counselors, one for each continental area of the world. Their work is coordinated and supervised by the Counselors serving at the International Teaching Center, which is located at the Bahá'í World Center in Haifa, Israel, and functions under the guidance of the Universal House of Justice.

The institutions of the Bahá'í Administrative Order are critical to the promotion of peace. They foster, support, and give direction to the sustained efforts of the Bahá'í community as they engage in the necessary educational and service activities designed to transform values and build capacities essential to creating a culture of peace. They also promote and contribute to the social, material, and spiritual well-being of society and the attainment of peace. As the Bahá'í community increases in size and its members and institutions develop the necessary capacities, they progressively engage with the wider community in efforts to deal with the problems confronting society.[38] They "enter into collaboration, as their resources permit, with an increasing number of movements, organizations, groups and individuals, establishing partnerships that strive to transform society and further the cause of unity, promote human welfare, and contribute to world solidarity."[39] Moreover, under the guidance of the Universal House of Justice, the elected and appointed institutions at all levels collaborate with each other and with the community and individuals to advance a grassroots process of community building worldwide.

Principles Key to the Promotion of Peace

Other key principles advanced by Bahá'u'lláh as the means to reinforce progress toward peace, include the full equality between women and men, and the elimination of all forms of prejudice—racial, class, religious, political, national, and economic. Peace is impossible without the eradication of the evil perpetrated by prejudice. Entrenched racial prejudice blocks opportunities and the expression of individual capacities. Economic prejudice and discrimination create disparities in the distribution of income and wealth among individuals and countries. Prejudice in the political sector can divide people based on their adherence to ideologies and conflicting values resulting from "liberal" and

23

"conservative" worldviews. Likewise, nationalism as opposed to patriotism can result in movements that divide groups against each other based on ideology, ethnicity, religious affiliation, and the like. Those who are the perpetrators of prejudice spread attitudes and behaviors that foment corruption, arrogance, and oppression. As prejudice is allowed expression and is tolerated in the social order, the attainment of peace becomes impossible. Prejudice promotes dissension, fuels hatred, and exposes the malicious side of human nature that when unleashed results in heinous acts of barbarity. The Bahá'í Writings place a strong emphasis on bringing an end to all forms of prejudice, especially racism, so that the major barriers to peace can be eliminated. "Until all these barriers erected by prejudice are swept away," explain the Bahá'í teachings, "it is not possible for humanity to be at peace."[40]

Bahá'u'lláh explained that the purpose of religion "is to safeguard the interests and promote the unity of the human race, and to foster the spirit of love and fellowship."[41] Religion is intended to foster the moral and spiritual progress of humanity and civilization. However, Bahá'u'lláh explains that religion must agree with science and reason. "Arts, crafts, and sciences," wrote Bahá'u'lláh, "uplift the world of being, and are conducive to its exaltation. Knowledge is as wings to man's life, and a ladder for his ascent."[42] The importance of the complementary nature of religion and science, both functioning as different systems of knowledge that facilitate the human perception of reality, is elucidated in the following extracts from talks delivered by 'Abdu'l-Bahá:

> Any religious belief which is not conformable with scientific proof and investigation is superstition, for true science is reason and reality, and religion is essentially reality and pure reason; therefore, the two must correspond. Religious teaching which is at variance with science and reason is human invention and imagination unworthy of acceptance, for the antithesis and opposite of knowledge is superstition born of the ignorance of man. If we say religion is opposed to science, we lack

knowledge of either true science or true religion, for both are founded upon the premises and conclusions of reason, and both must bear its test.[44]

As was mentioned above, Bahá'u'lláh called for the achievement of full equality of women and considered it as a central requirement for the achievement of peace. He also promoted universal education as the means toward promoting freedom of thought, the expansion of the mind, the advancement of knowledge, and the elimination of superstition and prejudice. He stated that an auxiliary international language, in addition to one's native tongue, would serve as a mechanism for world unity in that it would greatly enhance communication and consultation. He identified work performed in the spirit of service as a spiritual virtue, and strongly upheld the principle of unity in diversity. The spirit and purpose of the principle is to guard against attempts to "suppress the diversity of ethnical origins, of climate, of history, of language and tradition, of thought and habit, that differentiate the peoples and nations of the world. It calls for a wider loyalty, for a larger aspiration than any that has animated the human race."[45]

Together, these principles, along with the institutions described above that are established on the international, national, regional, and local level, administer the affairs of the Bahá'í community. They are responsible for the emerging new world order of Bahá'u'lláh, which conforms to the imperative needs of the current period in the evolving history of humanity. The spiritual teachings and institutions of His world order all have one goal in common— that of translating spiritual, moral principles into action in the promotion and realization of world peace. Peace is the ultimate intended aim of His religion.

Promoting the Well-Being of Humanity

The mission of the Faith of Bahá'u'lláh is to establish world unity and to usher in an age of peace. The achievement of this transformative mission involves not only a profound change in human values—the emergence of a deep and abiding appreciation of the oneness and wholeness of humankind—but also the emergence of global institutions necessary for the establishment of just and unified relationships between the peoples and nations of the world. War must be eliminated and universal peace firmly established. This far-reaching vision of the future of humanity, set out in the Bahá'í Writings, is referred to as the World Order of Bahá'u'lláh.[46] The Bahá'í Administrative Order constitutes the first shaping of the future World Order. It represents the "nucleus" and "pattern" of a new social order destined to bring about the unification of humankind.[47] Its laws and institutions are "destined to be a pattern for future society, a supreme instrument for the establishment of the Most Great Peace and the one agency for the unification of the world, and the proclamation of the reign of righteousness and justice upon the earth."[48]

Bahá'ís understand that their Faith and its Administrative Order have an important role to play in the process of creating a united and peaceful world, and they confidently work to establish the future World Order. However, Bahá'ís do not believe that the new Order will be brought into existence solely through their own efforts or the influence of their faith. In building for the future, they also seek to actively collaborate with peoples and organizations who are committed to the principle of the oneness of humankind and who are working to uphold human rights. Bahá'ís acknowledge the important steps taken by the League of Nations and the United Nations toward the emergence of a system of global governance based on justice, and they recognize that the achievement of such ends requires stages in the adjustment of national and international political attitudes, and in the accepted and enforceable principles regulating the relationships between nations.

The Bahá'í teachings indicate that the unfoldment of World Order will occur in an evolutionary manner and will be associated with the gradual emergence of peace: First, progress towards the World Order will be marked by the establishment of the Lesser Peace, a form of political peace entered into by the nations through international agreement. The Bahá'í teachings envisage that the Lesser Peace will emerge from the suffering and social upheavals of the contemporary world. According to Hatcher and Martin, "The fundamental feature of the Lesser Peace is the establishment of international safeguards to prevent the recurrence of war among nations. These safeguards would be explicitly outlined in a formal agreement supported by all the nations of the earth, and based on the principle of 'collective security' according to which all the nations should arise collectively to suppress any aggressor nation."[49]

At a later stage, the Lesser Peace will evolve into the Most Great Peace. It is envisioned that the advent of the Most Great Peace will coincide with the emergence of the World Order of Bahá'u'lláh, and that the fruit of this great World Order will be the birth and efflorescence of a world civilization, described by Shoghi Effendi as "the child of the Most Great Peace and hallmark of the Golden Age of the Dispensation of Bahá'u'lláh."[50] All these will come about as a result of the gradual recognition of Bahá'u'lláh's mission by the peoples of the world and by the acceptance and application of the principles contained in His revelation. Anticipating the depth of such changes, Shoghi Effendi writes, "The Most Great Peace . . . as conceived by Bahá'u'lláh—a peace that must inevitably follow as the practical consequence of the spiritualization of the world and the fusion of all its races, creeds, classes and nations—can rest on no other basis, and can be preserved through no other agency, except the divinely appointed ordinances that are implicit in the World Order that stands associated with His Holy Name."[51]

The transformations necessary to build the World Order of Bahá'u'lláh will require centuries of dedicated effort, both on the individual and collective level. Its tasks are challenging and multifaceted—from understanding the vision of the oneness of the human family to transforming human values and systems of governance and creating opportunities for peace to emerge.

Undeterred by the challenges involved, the members of the Bahá'í Faith are actively taking conscious steps to bring the vision closer to realization through developing the capacities of their administrative institutions to minister to the needs of humanity and through engaging in collaborative learning and sharing experiences with like-minded individuals and movements committed to upraising the well-being and prosperity of humankind.

From the earliest days of the Faith to the present, the history of the development of the worldwide Bahá'í community and its administrative institutions provides concrete examples of the community's commitment and systematic approach to engaging in learning how to increase capacity to build cohesive communities and to nurture the processes associated with the emergence of peace. The community continues to collaborate with organizations, individuals, and movements to build a unity of vision and action toward promoting the well-being of all people and to advance ideas toward global security and peace. Additional information on this subject is readily available. In this volume, however, we will focus on the unique contribution of the life and work of 'Abdu'l-Bahá in the pursuit of peace.[52]

In the following chapters, we will examine the actions of 'Abdu'l-Bahá to spread abroad the teachings of Bahá'u'lláh concerning peace. Inspired by the revelation of His Father, 'Abdu'l-Bahá devoted His life to furthering efforts to bring into existence a new international order. To this end, in 1875, during the reign of Náṣiri'd-Dín Sháh, He addressed to the rulers and people of Persia a treatise entitled *The Secret of Divine Civilization*, setting out the spiritual principles and practical means that must guide the shaping of their society in the age of human maturity. An astute observer of world events, 'Abdu'l-Bahá clearly predicted the outbreak of World War I. During His travels in the West in 1911–1912, He warned of the catastrophe He saw approaching. A leading Montreal newspaper contains the following report of 'Abdu'l-Bahá's words: "All Europe is an armed camp. These warlike preparations will necessarily culminate in a great war. The very armaments themselves are productive of war. This great arsenal must go ablaze. There is nothing of the nature of a prophecy about such a view . . . it is based on reasoning solely."[53]

The Bahá'í Faith and Peace: Principles of an Integrated, Holistic Peace

From His extensive Writings and correspondence, it is evident that, throughout His life, 'Abdu'l-Bahá was keenly interested in universal peace and in fostering the means for its accomplishment. We will explore the means by which 'Abdu'l-Bahá enhanced the understanding of the members of the Bahá'í community about peace and examine the systematic approach He used to promulgate the message of peace to the world at large. We will describe His contact with leaders of thought and peace groups during His travels in the West and His involvement in the discourses of society; consider the contribution of the Tablets of the Divine Plan to the promotion of peace; and study the historic letters He wrote to the Executive Committee of the Central Organization for a Durable Peace at The Hague.

3 / Signs of the Times—Historical Context for War and Peace

The Revelation of Bahá'u'lláh diagnoses the condition of human society and prescribes the necessary remedy to enable humanity to take the next step in its unfolding destiny. Bahá'u'lláh states that, since "Every age hath its own problem, and every soul its particular aspiration," it follows that "The remedy the world needeth in its present-day afflictions can never be the same as that which a subsequent age may require." He therefore calls attention to the necessity of reading the social reality and understanding the state of the world and advises, "Be anxiously concerned with the needs of the age ye live in, and center your deliberations on its exigencies and requirements."[1]

This chapter introduces some of the forces for social and cultural change in the years leading up to World War I that were sweeping across the globe, competing for attention and influence, reorienting worldviews, challenging traditional customs and values, and impacting the lives of peoples throughout the world. It also briefly describes the primary factors leading to the outbreak of the First World War. The following chapter will examine the activities of the European peace movements in their efforts to prevent another outbreak of war and to set in place conditions for a sustainable peace.

The last twenty-five years of the eighteenth century saw a series of social, political, and economic upheavals that permanently altered the character of the western world. In Europe and North America, old sovereignties were

31

overthrown and new political structures—the American Republic, revolutionary France—were erected in their place. And in England, the rise of industry began to reshape the practices by which men and women had lived since the dawn of history.[2]

Throughout the eighteenth and nineteenth centuries, the world witnessed a relentless British and European drive to control territories all over the globe. Colonies not only provided direct supplies of valuable natural resources and manpower but were also a theater of conflict in which Europe's antagonisms were played out. In the post-Napoleonic era, a political system of alliances was put in place in 1815 at the Congress of Vienna to preserve the influence of the Great Powers—Russia, Prussia, Austria, and Great Britain. While the congress maintained European accord for a period of time, it ultimately led to the intensification of rivalries and competition for preeminence between nations—both within Europe and beyond—and it motivated nations to consolidate empires and enhanced the scramble for trade routes and colonies.

During the Imperial Age, Spain, Britain, France, Germany, the Netherlands, Portugal, Italy—and to a lesser extent, Denmark and Sweden—were all involved in the competition for territories. Colonies often started off as trading posts, in places such as India, but through political maneuvering and exercising military might, European countries began to take control. People living in the Americas, Africa, India, and Southeast Asia were often subjected to racial prejudice and political oppression. Economic exploitation of colonial territories occurred, as raw materials were exported out of the country, and slave labor was used. This situation persisted until after World War II, when many colonies around the world began to demand their independence.

The Dutch historian Johan Huizinga (1872–1945), known for his famous work *The Autumn of the Middle Ages*, made the following comment about history as a process. "In history, as in nature," he observed, "the processes of death and birth are eternally in step with one another. Old forms of thought die out while, at the same time and on the same soil, a new crop begins to bloom."[3] The statement could not be more relevant in explaining the changes and transformations that were taking place in Western Europe and Anglo-America as the nineteenth century gave way to the twentieth. It was a period of radical and world-shaking social change. The sweeping influence of modernization, the forces of rapid industrialization, and the eruption of creativity, new ideas, inventions, and technological advances all impacted the social and political order. The features and characteristics that defined this unique period in history ultimately unfolded within the landscape "of the world from which the Great War came."[4]

By any measure, the quality and rate of change that was in the air and on the ground around the turn of the nineteenth century was staggering. It was as if every tradition, institution, norm, idea, belief, and habit was being challenged by the heaviness of pressure imposed by a rushing flood of change. Change was everywhere, and it was rapid. One writer observed that the "fixity of the nineteenth century had vanished, yet change brought with it a mixture of excitement and anxiety."[5] The prominent historian Barbara Tuchman observed that 1890 to 1914 "was above all the culmination of a century of the most accelerated rate of change in man's record."[6] Tuchman captured the velocity of change by observing how a man in the Nineteenth Century "used his own and animal power, supplemented by that of wind and water, much as he had entered the Thirteenth, or, for that matter the First. He entered the Twentieth with his capacities in transportation, communication, production, manufacture and weaponry multiplied a thousand fold by the energy of machines."[7]

By the mid-nineteenth century, Europe had undergone major changes that affected people's beliefs about themselves. For example, the French Revolution not only advanced the notions of liberty, equality, and fraternity, it also introduced the idea of the nation-state as an organizing concept for politics, and the Napoleonic Wars (1803–1815) showed the strength of the nation-state. Likewise, the Industrial Revolution changed how people worked and acquired goods, the number of goods in circulation, and the economic relationship between industrialized and non-industrialized regions of the world. In addition, the rise of Liberalism strengthened a belief in progress and change; art and religion adapted to the new emphasis on materialism; and new techniques for communication and organization gave rise to the concept of "the masses" as a political and economic force.[8]

The Challenge of the New

The twentieth century, one of the most tumultuous periods in human history, was marked by numerous upheavals, revolutions, and radical departures from the past. Scientific discoveries and new social insights spurred many progressive social, economic, and cultural transformations. The way was cleared for new definitions of human rights and affirmations of personal dignity, expanded opportunities for individual and collective achievement, and bold new avenues for the advancement of human knowledge and consciousness. The collapse of old institutions on the one hand and the blossoming of new ways of thinking on the other has, during the last hundred years, given rise to the emergence of a trend toward an ever-increasing interdependence and integration of humanity.

Invention and Technology

In early 1901, the Western world was thriving economically and was experiencing unprecedented levels of economic growth, integration, and interdependence, creating a charged and stimulating environment that liberated the human mind. New ideas were in motion and spreading in every direction. Inventions and new devices brought greater ease to daily living and, at the same time, accelerated the pace of life. The introduction of new technologies impacted and disrupted almost every aspect of daily existence and transformed cultural patterns. For instance, the introduction of the automobile increased the number of pedestrian accidents. The speed of the automobile startled foot-travelers who were accustomed to the slower and more predictable horse-drawn carriages and wagons. The underground train system laid out in London expanded its network by opening new lines every few years, which allowed passengers easier access to distances and locations not previously possible. Huge ships, both military and civilian, made for more efficient and speedier intercontinental and transcontinental travel. Expanding rail lines linked territories, shortened travel time, offered reliable transport and flexibility of movement for people and goods.

Regarding the rapidity with which every aspect of life was being transformed during the early 1900s, the historian Eric Hobsbawm noted that the world "was now genuinely global. Almost all parts of it were now known and more or less adequately or approximately mapped."[9] The telegraph and telephone eliminated the physical distance between two geographic locations. The newly established global postal service enabled widespread deliveries of all types of goods, supplies, and information. Deliveries of commodities and supplies even showed up at the consumer's door. The historian Niall Ferguson described how in 1901, the more affluent inhabitants of London "could have ordered a sack of coal from Cardiff, a pair of kid gloves from Paris or a box of cigars from Havana."[10]

The Industrial Age was penetrating every facet of life, as well as social, economic, and cultural interactions. Historian Philipp Blom described the public's reaction to electricity when it was displayed at the enormous Palais d'Electricité, at the World Fair in Paris, in 1900. Millions of people "flocked to see the miracle of tens of thousands of light bulbs turning night into day, and lending mysterious colours to the grand fountain in front of the building."[11] The Paris World Fair also featured the largest exhibits of weapons of war—the British-made fully automatic Vickers-Maxim machine gun and the French-made Creusot long-range cannon. Barbara Tuchman provided the following comments written by a correspondent who saw the exhibit: "An English correspondent . . . moved to philosophize on the real meaning of the Exposition for the new era it introduced. Schneider's great gun seemed to him to hold the world collected in Paris under its threat and to mark the passage of war from a realm of sport to a realm of science in which the making of weapons absorbed the ingenuity of mankind. If the lull ever came, he wrote, the arts of peace might revive, 'but meanwhile the Paris Exhibition has taught us that the triumph of the modern world is purely mechanical.'"[12]

Other inventions included moving pictures that, in addition to featured films, became a new medium for the spread of news and information. The typewriter increased production efficiency in businesses, government offices, banks, and even for famous writers. In the United States, Mark Twain became the first author who submitted a typewritten book manuscript.[13] Newspapers and periodicals were disseminated near and far. In the 1890s, *Lloyd's Weekly* in the United Kingdom printed one million copies, and by 1900, the same number of copies were printed for the French newspaper *Le Petit Parisien.*

The Scientific Revolution

"There are times," wrote the historian Hobsbawm, "when man's entire way of apprehending and structuring the universe is transformed in a fairly brief period of time, and the decades which preceded the First World War were one of these."[14] In physics and mathematics, a revolution occurred as existing theories could no longer explain the new observations and emerging theories. For instance, Max Planck's quantum theory was a major leap forward in theoretical physics, as was Albert Einstein's theory of relativity, and Ernest Rutherford's discoveries in radioactivity and nuclear physics. The discovery of germ theory, by the works of Louis Pasteur (microbiologist and chemist), Joseph Lister (surgeon), and Robert Koch (physician), transformed the field of medicine by linking diseases to microorganisms that were detectable only by the microscope.

A new generation of educated and intellectual men and a few women were challenging the prevailing practices and beliefs found in the arts and sciences of the previous century. A small number of accomplished women penetrated fields previously restricted to men. Among them was Marie Curie, who in 1903 received her doctoral degree from the Faculté des Sciences in Paris. In her doctoral thesis, she explained her discovery of a new element "with very curious properties."[15] What Curie had contributed to science was an understanding of the phenomenon of radioactivity. Her bold and meticulous scientific experiments won her and her collaborators the Nobel Prize in Physics in 1903. Initially, the Nobel Prize was awarded to her husband, Pierre Curie and their colleague Antoine Henri Becquerel. However, her husband refused to accept the award and explained to the committee that it was primarily through the significant contributions made by Marie Curie that the discovery of radioactivity came to be. Eight years later in 1911, Marie Curie was awarded a second Nobel Prize in Chemistry for her discovery of two elements, radium and polonium.

Philipp Blom described the full reach and influence of scientific thought and technology on people's everyday life at the start of the twentieth century: "While the world was attacked, ridiculed, reshaped and questioned on a conceptual, fundamental level which was understood only by a few brilliant minds, the scientific recasting of reality also had very palpable effects, reaching into the daily lives and imaginations of ordinary people. The burst of scientific discovery during the nineteenth century now pushed technology into every area of human experience."[16]

The processes impacting the world potentially can have positive and negative outcomes. For example, discoveries in the fields of biology and genetics—disciplines that influence social and political aspects of society—had a fundamental impact on the spread of nonscientific ideas regarding the "racial" classification of human beings. In his 1901 Huxley lecture, Sir Francis Galton, a cousin to Charles Darwin and considered the founding father of eugenics, spoke about "The possible improvement of the human breed under the existing conditions of law and sentiment." He explained, "The possibility of improving the race of a nation depends on the power of increasing the productivity of the best stock. This is far more important than that of repressing the productivity of the worst. . . . In seeking for the improvement of the race we aim at what is apparently possible to accomplish. . . . To no nation is a high human breed more necessary than to our own, for we plant our stock all over the world and lay the foundation of the dispositions and capacities of future millions of the human race."[17]

Charles Darwin's theory of evolution and the philosophy of eugenics helped fuel racist ideologies about the natural inferiority of certain human populations. Natural selection, or what became known as social Darwinism, identified species as the unit of selection and races as social categories corresponding to species eugenics. Eugenics and social Darwinism attributed what were viewed at the time as inferior human social traits to nature or to biological differences between human beings. Friedrich Nietzsche, German philosopher and cultural critic, supported eugenic ideas, writing about breeding higher level human beings or of transforming a man into a superman. Certain groups, such as the poor, were thought to be born inferior. Racist ideologies strongly supported the political program of colonialism. Later, in the aftermath of World War I, such commonly held racist beliefs influenced not only the outcome of the first war but would resurface during WWII, on a significantly larger and more evil scale.[18] Colonial soldiers from the five continents served in the Western Front of WWI.[19] A senior officer who was responsible for the training of West African soldiers wrote in a letter "that African soldiers were 'cannon fodder, who should, in order to save whites' lives, be made use of much more intensively.'"[20]

Historian Richard Fogarty explained:

By the early 20th century, thinking about race was moving toward a more biological understanding of human difference and its significance, with an emphasis on physical features such as colour. But earlier conceptions of racial difference had not disappeared completely, and it was common during World War One for Europeans to speak of national or ethnic differences in terms of race. For instance, many believed that the war pitted the English and French "races" against the Germanic, or Teutonic, "race." Another area where this kind of national or ethnic understanding of race played a role was in the Balkans, where the war began. Despite numerous similarities and centuries of mixing that created many commonalities among the peoples of the region, ethnic differences loomed large in the self-understandings of many. Ethnic tension and nationalist aspirations helped ignite the war in 1914, when Serbian nationalists assassinated the heir to the throne of the Austro-Hungarian Empire, and these same factors were paramount in American President Woodrow Wilson's calls for national self-determination during the war and at the Paris Peace Conference in 1919.[21]

World War II saw the systematic murder of millions of innocent civilians, mostly the millions from the Jewish population, newborn children with serious defects, mental patients, the Romano (Gypsies), and "other 'racially foreign' elements still mingling with the *Volk* (ethnic Germans)."[22]

The Arts

The art scene of the period, confronted with the desire to push the boundaries of art and to capture the radical changes in the current mood of society, was also undergoing a profound transformation. Among the artists who led the change movement were those who had their pulse on the new emerging industrial world with its undercurrents of alienation, disorder, and dissention—its glaring injustices that fueled the rising tide of rebellion among the poor working-class people.

In London, painter and critic Roger Fry opened an exhibition called "Manet and the Post-Impressionist" at the Grafton Galleries in 1910. Most of the paintings on display were those of Paul Gaugin, Vincent van Gogh, and Paul Cézanne, together with the works of Georges-Pierre Seurat, Pablo Picasso, and Henri Matisse. The artists featured in the display were among the first who seemed to have accurately read the barometer of change that was slowly fashioning the rise of a different and unfamiliar world. Unconstrained by traditional popular art forms of the day, this new band of painters used every brush-stroke to capture raw human emotion—such as the suffering of the common people, passion, and sensuality—in an explosion of color that went beyond the norm of the calculated, conventional "realistic" art of the day. The Post-Impressionists indulged in bright colors, and they introduced new abstract forms to which the status quo aesthetics of the time reacted with outrage and mockery. The reaction of the critics and public to the paintings in the exhibit signaled one of the most important moments in the history of modern art.

To the majority of those who attended the exhibit in London, the paintings were considered an affront, an insult to everything that art was meant to be.[23] And yet in Germany, the art critic Julius Meier Graefe recognized the genius of Gaugin's art "in terms of disease and civilization, health and nature, virility and femininity."[24] Indeed, art historian and critic Waldemar Januszczak observed that in Gaugin's art, one sees that the painter "wished for less civilization and more meaning in life. He was in search of something worth believing in and prepared to go anywhere to find it."[25]

Among Roger Fry's circle of friends who attended the exhibit in London was the artist and designer Vanessa Bell and painter Duncan Grant. Their reaction to the paintings was one of enthusiasm, elation, and inspiration. Virginia Woolf, also at the exhibit, was clearly touched by what she saw. The imprint of post-Impressionism art on Woolf would find expression in her future literary works. In her essay "Mr. Bennett and Mrs. Brown," where she explored modernism and fiction, Woolf wrote, "And now I will hazard a second assertion, which is more disputable perhaps, to the effect that on or about December 1910 *human character changed* (italics added)."[26] It was Fry who had come up with the brilliant title for the exhibit, and although he was harshly judged and derided by London society, he nevertheless eventually achieved what he had set out to accomplish. He had succeeded in introducing new ideas that influenced and changed British art and culture. Eventually, Post-Impressionist art significantly influenced major modern art movements such as Cubism, Art Nouveau, and German Expressionism.

Architecture

For the great empires, exterior appearances of wealth, power, and display were important, and this included the architectural style of buildings. Such grand structures were particularly held in high regard by the emperor of the Hapsburg Empire. Similarly, the Austro-Hungarian monarchy erected buildings that portrayed symbols of order and stability, of security and permanence. In Vienna, there were a series of beautifully constructed classical buildings commensurate with the empire's history, style, image, and purpose. Gothic, neo-Baroque, Hellenic, and neo-Renaissance majestic architectural structures, commissioned by Emperor Franz Joseph in May 1865, lined the city's grand boulevard, Ringstrasse. The imposing works of architecture that lined the boulevard were a veneer, a façade intended to convey power and unwavering authority to the surrounding rival empires. The external appearance of these structures concealed the fact that the Austro-Hungarian Empire was economically trailing behind its European neighbors and was tormented by internal and external competing powers. None of this was exposed, and all of it was carefully concealed.

By the turn of the century, architecture, like art, was in rapid transition and moving away from previous architectural structures. A whole generation of architects began to develop new designs where structures were functional, exposed (lacking ornamentation), and had purity of line. Among the architects were Adolf Loos (1870–1933) and Otto Wagner (1841–1918), both of whom lived in Vienna. Loos, among others, was influenced by the British designer William Morris (1834–1896), who founded the Art Nouveau Arts and Craft Movement. For a time, Loos worked at Louis Sullivan's architectural office in Chicago, where he was exposed to designs of the first skyscrapers to be constructed in the world. Other architects who were part of the functionalism movement included Hendrik Petrus Berlage (1856–1934) in Amsterdam, who founded modern Dutch architecture with its emphasis on community and practical aesthetics. Berlage was significantly influenced by Frank Lloyd Wright during the final phase of his architectural style, and in 1934, he designed the Haags Gemeentemuseum, which was built in The Hague.[27]

The changes in architectural design were radical in comparison to the conventional norms. The impact of architectural style within a changing social order was no less radical than what had been projected by the canvases displayed at the Post-Impressionists exhibit in London. The new art and architecture conveyed a message against bourgeois morality, a view espoused by Friedrich Hegel, among others, that suggested that conflict and war are the forces behind historical progress. This view represented a form of social Darwinism and a cyclical theory of history that believed wars were crucial for humanity's progress. According to this theory, the stronger, superior people won wars and imposed their culture to create a new civilization, until another group came along to force a new civilization on the old.[28] The tensions in architecture, art, and other forces of social change revealed the conflict that was intensifying between the forces of modernity and tradition.

Status of Women

One of the most significant social changes to occur in the pre-war years was in relation to the role and status of women. Among middle class women predominantly in Britain, but also in other European countries and in the United States, the courageous suffragettes and some suffragists rose against a strong male hierarchy in organizing campaigns to win the right to vote and promote women's emancipation. For the first time in European history, more women were receiving an education and making their own money. For both working and middle-class women, opportunities for employment and income provision increased. A notable change took place in the growth of occupations for women in offices and shops. For example, in Britain, 7,000 women in 1881 were employed by the central and local government, as compared to 76,000 in 1911. For the same time period, the number of commercial and business clerks rose from 6,000 to 146,000, in large part due to the invention of the typewriter.[29] In Germany, the number of women employed as shop assistants grew from 32,000 in 1882 to 174,000 in 1907. By the late 1800s, women in Europe were giving birth to fewer children. Although the decline in birth rates was partly due to the decline in infant mortality rates, it does not fully explain the transition to lower birthrates. Lower birthrates also meant that women were marrying later.

The changes taking place in the lives of women also had a profound impact on the lives of men. The traditional world of pre-industrial-age masculine characteristics was, in their eyes, under siege. Machines were replacing muscle power. The mind and intellect were replacing manual skills. Power—as manifested through bodily strength, manliness, and features of the warrior—was no longer the norm. "Men reacted with an aggressive restatement of the old values," Blom noted. He explained, "Never before had so many uniforms been seen on the street or so many duels fought, never before had there been so many classified advertisement for treatments allegedly curing 'male maladies' and 'weak nerves'; and never before had so many men complained of exhaustion and nervousness, and found themselves admitted to sanatoriums and even mental hospitals."[30]

The decline in birthrates was also viewed as an omen of the declining status as perceived by men. Anxiety grew among the elite class—the white "civilized" people of Europe—about the higher breeding rates for colonial and lower-class populations. Despite such expressions of unease and tensions, with overtones of racism, the women of Europe were challenging the status quo. They were questioning Western conventional cultural values set in the rigid system of patriarchy. Indeed, the old norms and values were incongruous in the ever-changing, evolving society. In less than a generation, the lives of women, whether feminist or not, changed in large part because of education, work, and the choice of having fewer children.

Social Inequality—Race, Class, and Poverty

Misogyny, anti-Semitism, and racism were prominent features of the strong reaction that arose in response to the rapid social change taking place in European society. Women were accused of abolishing traditional values, including failing to fulfil their role as child-bearer. Jews were falsely perceived as becoming economically powerful and thus a threat to the economy. The colonial populations had higher birthrates than the Europeans and were viewed as being genetically inferior. In his seminal book, *The Souls of Black Folk*, W. E. B. Du Bois wrote, "The problem of the twentieth century is the problem of the color-line—the relation of the darker to the lighter races of men in Asia and Africa, in America and the islands of the sea."[31]

At the turn of the century, unemployment among industrial workers was a constant threat. There were trade unions whose purpose was to protect the workers. However, these unions were without sufficient resources and lacked the rights to be able to safeguard workers' social security. The trade unions were becoming more and more aggressive as they challenged the economic status quo. Among the middle classes there was growing awareness and reaction to the dismal condition of the workers and the poor.

In the following extract, Tuchman provides a vivid window into the dismal life of the poor working class, not only in Great Britain but throughout the empires of Europe:

They came from the warrens of the poor, where hunger and dirt were king, where consumptives coughed and the air was thick with the smell of latrines, boiling cabbage and stale beer, where babies wailed and couples screamed in sudden quarrels, where roofs leaked and unmended windows let in the cold blasts of winter, where privacy was unimaginable, where men, women, grandparents and children lived together, eating, sleeping, fornicating, defecating, sickening and dying in one room, where a tea-kettle served as a wash boiler between meals, old boxes served as chairs, heaps of found straw as beds, and boards propped across two crates as tables, where sometimes not all the children in a family could go out at one time because there were not enough clothes to go round, where decent families lived among drunkards, wife-beaters, thieves and prostitutes, where life was a seesaw of unemployment and endless toil, where a cigar-maker and his wife earning 13 cents an hour worked seventeen hours a day seven days a week to support themselves and three children, where death was the only exit and the only extravagance and the scraped savings of a lifetime would be squandered on a funeral coach with flowers and a parade of mourners to ensure against the anonymity and last ignominy of Potter's field.[32]

Impact of Political Forces

During the first decade of the twentieth century, rumblings of social and political trouble in Europe began to grow. While the immediate precipitating event to the declaration of war was the assassination of Archduke Ferdinand in Sarejevo, there were many other factors that also played a role in leading up to World War I. Historians have identified a number of factors that contributed to the rivalry between the European Great Powers and allowed such a widespread conflict to break out. Indeed, historians continue to debate the cause of WWI.

Samuel R. Williamson, Jr, indicates that "Imperialism shaped almost every facet of international politics from 1898 to 1914."[33] Before the outbreak of the war, Europe's main powers were divided into two armed camps by a series of alliances. These were the Triple Alliance consisting of Germany, Austria-Hungary, and Italy (1882); and the Triple Entente of Britain, Russia, and France (1907). While the alliances were defensive in nature, a condition of the alliances was that, should a conflict break out between two countries, one from each of the opposing alliances, all the other countries, party to their respective alliance, were obligated to become involved in the conflict. Historian of the First World War A. J. P. Taylor observed that "The alliances created an excessively rigid diplomatic framework, within which relatively small detonators could produce huge explosions."[34]

Militarism was another of the long-term causes of the war. In the years prior to the war, military spending increased greatly among all the Great Powers. All except Britain had conscription. Over 85% of men of military age in France and 50% in Germany had served in the army or navy. France had the highest proportion of its population in the army, and the size of the armies of both France and Germany had more than doubled between 1870 and 1914. The rivalry between the powers led to a building up of weapons and an increase in distrust. After 1911, an armaments race set much of the agenda. In addition, colonial rivalry had led to a naval arms race between Britain and Germany, which seriously worsened relations between both countries. The British-German dispute also led to greater naval cooperation between Britain and France.

Allied to this growing militarism was an intense nationalism in most of the Great Powers. The complexity of the situation is illustrated by the following examples: In Germany, the policy of Weltpolitik, or the desire for a world power status, influenced political and economic decisions. In France, there was a strong desire for revenge over the loss of Alsace and Lorraine in the 1870 Franco-German war. In Britain, imperialism and support for the empire was very evident. The strength of such nationalism meant that there was little resistance to war among the peoples in these countries. Many welcomed what they thought would be a short, victorious war.

Between 1900 and 1914, there were three major crises between the Great Powers. These crises exposed the differences between the powers and reinforced the hostility between them. Two were over Morocco (1905, 1911) and the other was over the Austrian annexation of Bosnia (1908). The effects of these crises were a hardening of attitudes and an increase in distrust between the different European powers. It led to a strengthening of the different alliances.

Historians have also drawn attention to the influence of domestic political agendas on the actions of the Great Powers. The condition of the poor is linked to another development of the social climate during the years prior to World War I. On September 6, 1901, as President McKinley was shaking hands at the Pan-American Exhibition in Buffalo, New York, a young anarchist by the name of Leon Czolgosz shot him twice in the chest. McKinley died on September 14, and his vice president, Theodore Roosevelt, was sworn in as president. In the period of thirteen years between 1900 and 1913, "forty heads of states, politicians and diplomats were murdered, including four kings, six prime ministers and three presidents."[35] Two kings, one queen, two prime ministers, and the commander-in-chief of the Turkish Army were assassinated in the Balkans.[36] None of the leaders who were assassinated were despots. Tuchman explained the assassinations as acts of "desperate or deluded men"[37] who were calling attention to their movement. The anarchist movement had gained widespread support across Europe and in Great Britain. The ideology was centered on the overthrow of the "enemy"—the ruling class and the bourgeoisie.

Historians have also suggested that, in light of internal political considerations, the war might well have served the purpose of diverting attention from a number of pressing political and social issues, such as the threat of a civil war in Ireland, the crisis over income tax, and the length of military service in France, and the unpopularity of the Czar in Russia. Likewise, the concern about the rise of socialism in Germany, Austria, Russia, Italy, and France led the ruling class in some of these countries to hope that a short victorious war would put an end to class differences and reduce the support for socialism that threatened the existing order. Underlying the assumptions of all the Great Powers in the period immediately before the outbreak of the war was the belief that if a war did break out, it would be a short one. Many in Britain felt that the war would be over by Christmas.[38]

In his recent book, *World Order,* Henry Kissinger offers the following comment on the causes of the Great War: ". . . the war that overturned Western civilization had no inevitable necessity. It arose from a series of miscalculations made by serious leaders who did not understand the consequences of their planning, and a final maelstrom triggered by a terrorist attack . . . In the end, the military planning ran away with diplomacy. It is a lesson subsequent generations must not forget."[39]

The protagonists in World War I were Austria-Hungary, Germany, and Turkey; who were opposed by Russia, France, and Great Britain. Other countries, such as Japan, Italy, the United States, and many smaller nations joined the war on different sides. All these nations were armed, and conscription was introduced. In the view of historian, H. G. Wells, the governments of Europe were "inspired by antiquated policies of hate and suspicion," and given the scientific advances in modern weaponry, "found themselves with unexampled powers both of destruction and resistance in their hands. The war became a consuming fire round and about the world, causing losses both to victors and vanquished out of all proportion to the issues involved."[40]

The main fighting against Germany was along the Western front, in Belgium and northern France. It was there, in the view of leaders on both sides, that the war would be decided. The fighting, however, was protracted and bloody. For three and a half years, neither side advanced more than a few miles along the line of trenches, despite the use of new weapons such as poison gas and the introduction of tanks. The stalemate was not relieved until the spring of 1918, when the Germans were defeated and thrown back into Belgium.[41]

In addition to the military campaigns on the continent of Europe, battles took place at sea and in the air, and the fighting reached such places as Russia, Turkey, Iran, the Caucasus, Palestine, and Mesopotamia. Commenting on the scope of the warfare and its social impact, Wells refers to the vast size of the armies, and the organization of "entire populations . . . for the supply of food and munitions to the front," which gave rise to the "cessation of nearly every sort of productive activity except such as contributed to military operations." According to Wells, "All the able-bodied manhood of Europe was drawn into the armies and navies or into the improvised factories that served them."[42] As a consequence, nations were impoverished; peoples were socially uprooted and transplanted; and trade, shipping, and communications were disrupted.

The entry of the United States into the war on the side of the Allies in 1917 was a major turning point and hastened the end of the conflict. When the war finally came to an end in 1918, the allied powers imposed a vindictive peace treaty on their defeated enemies and demanded ruinous reparations of them. These actions not only served to plant the seeds of another more terrible conflict, but also helped "prepare demoralized peoples in Europe to embrace totalitarian promises of relief which they might not otherwise have contemplated."[43]

Assessing the long-term implications of the Great War, Eric Hobsbawm offers the sobering view that "the First World War began the descent into barbarism." In his judgment, this war "opened the most murderous era so far recorded in history"; and "the limitless sacrifices which governments imposed on their own men" as they drove them into tragic and wasteful battles "set a sinister precedent." Furthermore, he observes that "the very concept of a war of total national mobilization shattered the central pillar of civilized warfare," by blurring "the distinction between combatants and non-combatants," and he regards the pervasive tendency to demonize the enemy to governments' need to sustain the fighting focus of largely volunteer armies. Beyond its moral and psychological impact, Hobsbawm attests, "the Great War ended in social and political breakdown, social revolution and counter-revolution on an unprecedented scale;" the direct impact of this era of breakdown and revolution was to be felt for the next thirty years.[44]

In that fateful month of August, 1914, as the protagonists stood on the threshold of war, few predicted its catastrophic outcomes—that it was to lead to the fall of four great imperial dynasties (in Germany, Russia, Austria-Hungary, and Turkey) and result in the Bolshevik Revolution in Russia; that in its destabilization of European society, it would lay the groundwork for World War II; and that the ensuing conflict was destined to be characterized as "one of the greatest watersheds of 20th century geopolitical history."[45]

In the following chapter, we turn to a discussion of the movements towards peace in the years leading up to the war and in its aftermath as a context for considering 'Abdu'l-Bahá's unique contribution to furthering the discourse on issues associated with laying the foundations for a culture of peace.

4 / Movements toward Peace

An important feature of the intellectual and social landscape in the period leading up to World War I and after the outbreak of hostilities was the involvement of organizations and civil society in a wide range of activities promoting peace. One such group, created in 1915, after the world war had begun, was the Central Organization for a Durable Peace at The Hague, which actively formulated and promoted constructive ideas considered necessary for achieving and sustaining peace. It was to this organization that 'Abdu'l-Bahá addressed His historic letters.

As a context for studying 'Abdu'l-Bahá's communications with the Executive Committee of the Central Organization for a Durable Peace at The Hague, we briefly describe earlier attempts to create durable peace, including several significant peace gatherings that took place in The Hague, and examine, in some detail, the work and program of the Central Organization.

This chapter briefly reviews the movements toward peace, especially in Europe, in the years leading up to and during the war years. Special consideration is given to the movements toward peace prior to 1899, to the contribution of the international Peace Conferences at The Hague, and to the nature of peace activities that were pursued following the outbreak of war.

A World Without War

Historical Context

A peace movement in Europe had existed since the end of the Napoleonic Wars. Prior to that time, wars had largely been limited to armed confrontations between two nations and not a world conflagration. War was believed to be inevitable and the only way to settle certain disputes; and it was thought that it was man's nature to fight and that no durable peace was possible. While in the seventeenth and eighteenth centuries proposals for European Federation had been put forward, and in the nineteenth century, the idea of arbitration gained prominence, the first really organized efforts to maintain peace in Europe grew out of the Napoleonic wars.[1]

As mentioned in an earlier chapter, in the latter part of the nineteenth century, with the growth of the forces of nationalism and imperialism, war again broke out in Europe. The period after the Franco-Prussian war in 1870 was marked by the rise of nationalism and imperialism, which led to economic isolation, protection, and militarism. Militarism produced insecurity, and the peace of the world was only precariously maintained by defensive alliances and a balance of power. This same period was also marked by a countervailing trend forging mutual interdependence socially and economically. In 1874, for example, the Postal Union came into being, practically uniting the whole world in the matter of communication.[2]

Women were among the most active members in the peace movement in Europe. As they voiced their opposition to militarism, to the rapid arms race between the empires, and to the institution of war, politicians and newspapers mocked and ridiculed them. The Austrian Baroness Bertha von Suttner, who was awarded the Nobel Peace Prize in 1905 and who met 'Abdu'l-Bahá during His travels in America in 1912, was among the most active proponents for peace. She had witnessed firsthand the soldiers and civilians wounded in the Russo-Turkish War of 1877–78. Upon her return to Vienna, she wrote a book in opposition to war (*Die Waffen Nieder!*, "Put Down Your Arms"), which became a best seller. In a talk delivered in 1904, von Suttner spoke about the criminality of war: "Our opponents think that the wish to get rid of war is absurd, like the wish to get rid of death. Such a thing would truly be fine, but it is impossible, they say. Yet war is not death; it is murder. And not to murder someone is not an impossibility."[3]

Bertha von Suttner attended many peace congresses and conferences in Europe and the United States where she persistently voiced her frustrations about the lack of attention to the prevention and elimination of war on the part of the leaders of the world. Among other women who were active in the peace movement and wrote important works about the role of women in the abolition of war were feminists Rosa Mayreder in Vienna and Lida Gustava Heymann in Hamburg, Germany. Both were passionately opposed to war and active in the women's rights movement. Mayreder wrote, "The law of war, its most inner essence, is to destroy."[4] Heymann noted, "In the modern male state, women have not only been deprived of any possibility of expressing their essential nature, they had to submit to the male principle, they were forced to recognize it, they were raped."[5] All three women viewed war as a barbaric and homicidal institution. Throughout the pre-war period and after its outbreak, women continued to make unique contributions to the cause of peace. Further details will be provided in a later section of the chapter.

With the passage of time, the activities of the peace movement became better organized and more widespread. Two early initiatives, introduced in 1889, were the annual Universal Peace Congresses, attended by friends of peace from many countries, and the annual inter-parliamentary conferences established by lawmakers from several European countries to discuss major foreign policy questions and recommend measures to reduce tensions and foster reconciliation. The International Peace Bureau, set up in 1891, was one of the first programs aimed at cooperation within the peace movement at an international level. The Hague Peace Conferences of 1899 and 1907, described below, and the prospects for a third conference in 1915 were interpreted, optimistically, by peace workers as evidence of an emerging international spirit among nations. A survey conducted in early 1914 reported that the European peace movement comprised 190 peace societies, some with thousands of members, which published twenty-three periodicals in ten languages.[6]

The Hague International Peace Conferences, 1899 and 1907

The Hague's emergence as an international city of peace and justice is linked to the convening of two international peace conferences—the first in 1899 and the second in 1907. Called at the initiative of Czar Nicholas II of Russia, these gatherings, which are described in detail below, sought to set standards for the resolution of conflict between nations.

The first international peace conference was held in The Hague in 1899. It was the beginning of a special role for The Hague as an international city of peace and justice. The city subsequently became a permanent center of international law and the home of the historic Peace Palace, built in 1913 with an endowment from the American industrialist Andrew Carnegie. The Peace Palace now serves as the headquarters of both the International Court of Justice and the Permanent Court of Arbitration, a non-governmental organization at The Hague.

The Hague International Peace Conference, 1899

The 1899 Peace Conference at The Hague[7] was initiated by Czar Nicholas II of Russia with the objective of limiting armaments and military expenditure. It came at the end of a century whose numerous armed conflicts gave birth to the modern movements for arbitration, peace, and humanitarian law. Military powers, peace activists, arbitration proponents, and humanitarian organizations all had a role in shaping, in varying degrees, the outcome of the Conference. Peace societies began forming in the first decade of the nineteenth century in the wake of the war of 1812. The Napoleonic Wars in Europe and the American Civil War (1861–65) also gave rise to the early statements and codifications of the laws of war and humanitarian law. The Boxer Rebellion (1899–1901) in China, the three-month Spanish-American War (1898), which ended four centuries of Spanish influence in the Americas, and the 1898 Fashoda incident between France and Britain in the Egyptian Sudan reflected the tensions between and within the great European powers, whose shifting alliances in the 1880s and 1890s increased the sense that alternatives to war were needed. The broader context for each of these developments was the expanding industrialism at the turn of the century that made possible not only economic growth but a larger scale production and transport of armaments.[8]

In August 1898, Czar Nicholas II issued his famous invitation (also referred to as the Czar's Rescript) calling for international action to ensure "a real and lasting peace." "The Imperial Government," the invitation announced, ". . . believes that the present moment would be very favorable for seeking, by means of international discussion, the most effective means of ensuring to all peoples the benefits of a real and lasting peace, and above all of limiting the progressive development of existing armaments. . . . hundreds of millions are spent in acquiring terrible engines of destruction. National culture, economic progress, and the production of wealth are either paralyzed or perverted in their development."[9]

This statement was seized upon by the peace movement throughout the world as an opportunity for a great campaign for peace. Political organizations, peace groups, and churches were active in this movement. Individuals also made their contribution. W. T. Stead, the English editor and publisher, for example, spent four months touring European capitals demanding audiences with the national sovereigns and urging upon them the czar's proposal.[10]

The leaders of fifty-nine of the world's states were invited to send delegates to this unique peace conference. Representatives from twenty-six nations, the vast majority of whom were European, attended.[11] The Hague International Peace Conference of 1899 was noteworthy not only for its attempt to include participants from non-European countries, but also for the reason for its convocation—namely, to act as a restraint on war, to reduce the amount nations spent on armaments, and to ensure the benefits of a real and lasting peace to all peoples.

A World Without War

However, the 1899 Hague Peace Conference was not driven by the sudden conversion of Europe's rulers to pacifism but more by Russia's desire to escape the crushing burden of keeping up with the pace of Germany and England's acquisition of armaments in Western Europe. It was the czar's hope that armaments—land and naval—might be reduced and that the progressive development of existing armaments would be checked. James Tryon, the Assistant Secretary of the American Peace Society at the time, analyzed the contents and intention of the czar's invitation, as follows:

> The Rescript held up the maintenance of peace and possibility of reducing the expense of armaments as supreme ideals to which the governments, in response to the longing of the popular conscience for twenty years past, ought to direct their energies. Armaments were recognized as primarily the cause of the diversion of much labor and capital from productive to unproductive uses and of the creation of a crushing and growing financial burden upon the people, seriously injuring the public prosperity and checking the development of culture, progress and wealth, besides subjecting the nations to the danger of war from the mere massing of war materials ready for use.
>
> To meet this situation the Czar proposed a Conference at which the problem of peace and disarmament should be discussed by the governments. He believed that such a Conference would establish "the principles of justice and right, upon which repose the security of states and the welfare of peoples."[12]

The initial reaction of the nations to the czar's call to participate in a conference for the limitation of armaments was, in the words of historian Barbara Tuchman, one of "dazed wonderment liberally laced with distrust."[13] In a political climate of skepticism and suspicion, the czar was, "in some quarters, accused of trying to induce the world to disarm that he might take advantage of its helplessness; but, on the whole, people thought him sincere.

The fact that the document emanated from what was supposed to be the most military government in Europe made the document at once the more remarkable."[14]

The czar's invitation evoked an ambivalent response; nevertheless, news of its contents spread rapidly. "The Rescript at once became a theme of discussion throughout the world," due in part, to "the agitation of peace societies and the work of associations for the improvement of international law," which, according to Tryon, had, in recent years, "produced an effect upon the international consciousness." Civil society played a considerable role both before and after the first Hague conference. It served to influence public discourse, encourage consultation, and propose modifications to the agenda, which helped to overcome the initial reluctance of most governments to accept the czar's invitation.[15] The various peace societies kept up a veritable drum roll of urgings and entreaties. And, during the conference itself, the voice of the people made itself heard, with Belgium and The Netherlands, respectively, presenting petitions bearing 100,000 and 200,000 signatures.[16]

The Conference opened on May 18, 1899. It remained in session for two months and adjourned on July 29, 1899. It was attended by around one hundred male delegates, consisting of diplomats, professors of law, military and naval experts, and "men chosen for their fitness from the best equipped classes of the nations."[17] The topics for discussion included the limitation of armaments, the regulation of war, with restrictions upon certain kinds of explosives and engines of destruction, the application of the Geneva Convention of 1864 to naval war, and the employment of arbitration and mediation in the event of threatened war. The work was divided among three main commissions, each of which appointed several subcommittees to address specialized aspects of the business.[18]

The deliberations of the First Hague Peace Conference fell short of Czar Nicholas II's primary objective, the limitation of armaments. While endorsing in general terms the desirability of limiting the proliferation of armaments and restricting military budgets, the delegates were unable to agree on fixing the size of military forces and naval armaments or their budgets, and they failed to adopt instruments regarding the prevention of new types and calibers of rifles and naval guns.

The participants at the conference did, however, agree on the adoption of the following three conventions or treaties and three additional declarations.[19] The three conventions are: (1) The Convention for the Pacific Settlement of International Disputes, which included the creation of the Permanent Court of Arbitration, which is the oldest global institution for the settlement of international disputes; (2) The Convention for the Adaptation to Maritime Warfare of the Principles of the 1864 Geneva Convention, which resulted in the extension of protection to hospital ships and requires them to treat the wounded and shipwrecked sailors of all combatants regardless of allegiance; and, (3) The Convention relating to the Laws and Customs of War on Land, which specifies the treatment of prisoners of war, includes the provisions of the Geneva Convention of 1864 for the treatment of the wounded, and forbids the use of poisons, the killing of enemy combatants who have surrendered, looting of a town or place, and the attack or bombardment of undefended towns or habitations. Inhabitants of occupied territories may not be forced into military service against their own country, and collective punishment is forbidden.

The three conventions mentioned above, together with the Geneva Convention of 1864, are among the most important sources of twentieth and early twenty-first-century humanitarian law. Many of their provisions are still in force, and they have generated an enormous body of case law. The three declarations deal with (1) The Prohibition of the Use of Bullets which can Easily Expand or Change their Form Inside the Human Body such as Bullets with a Hard Covering which does not Completely Cover the Core or containing indentations; (2) The Prohibition of the Discharge of Projectiles and Explosives from Balloons or by Other New Analogous Methods: and, (3) The Prohibition of the Use of Projectiles with the Sole Object to Spread Asphyxiating Poisonous Gases.[20]

While the outcomes of the conference fell far short of the czar's original objective, its most important accomplishment was to contribute to institutionalizing the peaceful settlement of international disputes and to codifying and developing the rules of war. Assessing the work of the conference, legal expert A. Pearce Higgins, writing in 1909, judged its value in terms of "marking an important epoch in the development of international law." While acknowledging that "Almost before the ink on the Final Act was dry, war broke out between the South African republics and Great Britain," Higgins highlighted the importance of the conference's work in humanizing the laws of war both on land and sea, and its role in creating the Permanent Court of Arbitration at The Hague.[21]

Though in the Final Act, the summary document listing the major outcomes of the Peace Conference, the delegates had agreed to submit the three Conventions and Declarations to their governments for approval, states failed to live up to many of the goals and commitments of the 1899 Conference. Most states continued to increase military expenditures; while several nations brought cases to the Permanent Court of Arbitration, others turned to armed force (e.g. the Boer War 1899–1902, the Russo-Japanese War 1904–1905) to accomplish their aims rather than resorting to the peaceful means of dispute settlement established in Convention I (1899) of The Hague Peace Conference. Commenting on this situation, legal historian Madeline Doty noted that while arbitration and mediation were the prescribed methods of resolving conflict, implementation depended on the goodwill of the nations involved. Since the 1899 Conference had been unable to achieve a general treaty of obligatory arbitration, little could be done when nations refused to engage in arbitration. Taking a long-term perspective, Doty wrote, "Yet with all its defects, though no general treaty of obligatory arbitration was achieved, the first Hague Conference must be regarded as a milestone in the evolution of collaboration between nations and incidentally in the development of international law. . . . It was the first conference that accepted the free participation of all nations on equal terms without regard for race or creed. It was not of course a parliament but only a meeting of sovereign states which required unanimity for any rule to prevail."[22]

Despite its modest outcome, Tuchman noted that, at the end of the conference, the delegates did not seem ready "to bury the Hague idea." "However stunted their product," she observed, "most of them could not but feel a sense of having participated in something important and a desire that the foundations they had laid should not be lost. They registered the feeling in a 'Wish' for a Second Conference at some future date—although the idea did not please everyone."[23] This spirit of cautious optimism was shared by the wider public. According to Higgins, "men who were living in the autumn of 1899 realized that the nations at last had a system of peace."[24] It remained only to perfect that system through the action of successive Hague Conferences, and therefore the peace societies began to urge the calling of another conference.

The Hague International Peace Conference, 1907

A second Peace Conference[25] was held at The Hague in 1907 with a view to improving the 1899 Conventions, renewing the 1899 Declarations, and drafting a new convention on the laws and customs of maritime warfare. The agenda contained considerable unfinished matters left over from the Conference of 1899. The deliberations of the conference focused on three main areas: measures for the prevention of war; measures for the regulation of war; and measures relating to neutrality.

Forty-four States participated. In addition to those present at the 1899 gathering, the second conference was attended by delegates from the newly independent Norway and seventeen Latin American and Caribbean States, namely, Argentina, Bolivia, Brazil, Chile, Colombia, Cuba, the Dominican Republic, Ecuador, El Salvador, Guatemala, Haiti, Nicaragua, Panama, Paraguay, Peru, Uruguay, and Venezuela.

The treaties, declarations, and Final Act of the Second Conference were signed on October 18, 1907, and they came into force on January 26, 1910.

In all, the participants adopted thirteen separate conventions, or treaties, and one declaration. These documents were appended to the Final Act and open for the signature and ratification by all States in attendance. Three of the 1907 Conventions were revisions of those agreed to in 1899; six were related to naval operations.[26]

In many ways, the two Hague Peace Conferences provide vivid glimpses into States' evolving efforts to work out how to act and interact on a changing international stage. As in the case of the 1899 Conference, the 1907 Conference failed to take action upon the important question of the limitation of armaments, except to make it the subject of a resolution to be referred to the nations for further study. Nevertheless, the conference did manage to enlarge the machinery for voluntary arbitration and established conventions regulating the collection of debts, rules of war, and the rights and obligations of neutral nations. The Final Acts of the 1907 Conference were the unanimous acceptance by the delegates of the principle of compulsory arbitration and the stating of a number of *voeux* (resolutions), the first of which was the recommendation that another conference be summoned in eight years, thus establishing the concept that the best way to handle international problems was through a series of successive conferences. It was generally anticipated that the third Conference would take place in 1915.[27]

Writing in 1907, James L. Tryon, Assistant Secretary of the American Peace Society, provided the following optimistic assessment of the status of The Hague Peace Conferences:

> To sum up, The Hague peace system in a word is now important. The Hague conventions represent previously accepted or now generally agreed upon rules of International Law. The central feature of these conventions is that relating to the Pacific Settlement of International Disputes. By its terms, if war threatens, mediation, commissions of inquiry, or arbitration may be employed to prevent its occurrence. If war breaks out, mediation may stop it. But while it lasts its severities

upon enemies and infringements upon neutrals are restricted. The fact that the Conferences have become periodic, that their program will be more carefully arranged in the future than in the past, and that their procedure will be elaborated indicates their probable development into a real Parliament of Nations.

A Congress of Nations, when it comes, should be competent to deal with the most serious questions that arise between states and with the International Court ought to be a strong safeguard of international peace.[28]

Peace Movements at the Beginning of World War I

In the period from the first Hague Conference in 1899 to the outbreak of the war in 1914, peace organizations became respectable and even received public approval. The term *universal peace* was made acceptable by its use in The Hague Conferences, and governments became friendly to peace organizations. In the United States, for instance, two large peace foundations were created in 1910 and heavily endowed—the World Peace Foundation and the Carnegie Endowment for International Peace. There was, however, a divergence of views among the advocates for a durable peace. While both sides advocated cooperation and arbitration, one group wanted enforcement of those principles only through the moral force of public opinion, while the more politically minded were trying to discover a system of sanctions that could, using force if necessary, enforce arbitration and prevent war. Nevertheless, both streams of thought believed that some sort of federation or league of nations was essential.[29]

Peace activism continued after the outbreak of the First World War. It took many forms and involved a wide variety of groups, including historic peace groups (such as Quakers), pacifists, groups expressing conscientious objection to military service, anticonscription groups, and organizations promoting neutral mediation of the war. However, the movement was riven with internal divisions and largely collapsed early in the war. Among the issues that dogged the unity of the peace movement was the desire of individual groups to retain their independence and control their right to determine the future direction of the peace movement.

In addition, traditional prejudices, cultural, and nationalistic attitudes also limited the efficacy of the peace movement. Characterizing the situation in continental Europe at the time, David Patterson identified one of the fundamental problems as follows:

> most peace reformers, while internationalist in their thinking, were also solid nationalists. The peace advocates on the continent mostly came from diverse middle class backgrounds, but even they could not entirely escape the deep-seated authoritarian traditions of political dominance and war they had inherited. Many Italian peace advocates, for example, had supported their nation's war of conquest against Turkey in 1911, and during the two Moroccan crises French and German pacifists revived their bitter disagreements over Germany's annexation of Alsace and Lorraine more than a generation earlier.[30]

Throughout Europe, the socialist movement, with its large and well-organized working class, might well have had the potential to provide a mass basis for social mobilization against militarism and war. Believing capitalism led inevitably to imperialism and war, socialists in the decade before 1914 became more actively interested in foreign policy issues. However, many middle-class peace workers were skeptical of socialists' analyses of the economic causes of the armament race and war or fearful of their emphasis on class conflict.

In the decade leading up to the war, the British peace movement was thriving. Peace societies had expanded rapidly in number and membership, and in 1909, the disparate groups created the National Peace Council to coordinate their activities. The movement was initially united in its rejection of balance of power politics and entangling alliances; however, the membership was moved by the government's emotional argument that Britons had a moral responsibility to come to the aid of Belgium, a largely defenseless nation, whose neutrality had been assured by international treaty, in the face of German invasion. When the British Parliament declared war on August 4, 1914, the British peace movement split apart, but later reorganized around such issues as conscientious objection, conscription, and the promotion of programs designed to encourage neutral governments to bring the opposing sides together for a mediated settlement. In addition to promoting neutral mediation, initiatives such as the Union of Democratic Control (UDC), formed in September 1914, also stressed the imperative need for embedding principles of an enlightened "new diplomacy" in the peace settlement and the post-war world.[31]

Bertrand Russell (1872–1970), the British liberal philosopher, was, for some time, involved with the UDC.[32] In an article entitled "Is a Permanent Peace Possible?" written during the war years, Russell, an avowed pacifist, advocated both the establishment of some kind of international council to resolve disputes between nations in a just manner, and stressed the importance of mobilizing public opinion. He wrote:

> Far more important than any question of machinery is the problem of producing in all civilized nations such a horror of war that public opinion will insist upon peaceful methods of settling disputes. When this war ends, it is probable that every nation in Europe will feel such an intense weariness of the struggle that there will be little likelihood of a great war for another generation. The problem is, so to alter men's standards and outlook that, when the weariness has passed away, they shall not fall back into the old bad way, but shall escape from the nightmare into a happier world of free cooperation.[33]

The outbreak of hostilities was initially accompanied by a pro-war consensus in all the belligerent countries. This made it difficult for individuals and their groups to express doubts about the war or to advocate for peace. As the war continued, however, with no apparent end in sight, questions concerning the purposes of the war and the nations' peace aims emerged. In Britain, the continuing fighting and stalemate on the battlefields increasingly stimulated war weariness and thoughts of peace. The Union of Democratic Control, along with Quakers and many peace, socialist, labor, and women's groups, created a Peace Negotiations Committee, which circulated a petition describing the continuing war of attrition as a "moral iniquity, involving cruelty and suffering no words can describe" and calling on their government to seek early peace talks.[34]

In Germany, in the fall of 1914, the *Bund Neues Vaterland* (New Fatherland League) was founded in Berlin. The League set forth an internationalist program and hoped for a negotiated peace. Its members were primarily united in their opposition to ultranationalist annexation war aims. One who attended the New Fatherland League's weekly meetings was Albert Einstein (1879–1955), the outstanding German physicist, who, when war broke out, is reported to have commented, "We scientists in particular must foster internationalism."[35]

Increasingly, the European peace activists looked to the United States for support, since, at the outset of the war, Woodrow Wilson had offered his good offices. Following his reelection in 1916, Wilson offered to mediate with the contending parties to achieve an early settlement of the war. However, the offer had not gone very far when Germany abruptly announced all-out submarine warfare on January 31, 1917. The subsequent destruction of American merchant ships prompted Wilson to call for war against Germany, a call endorsed by Congress in early April 1917.[36]

Establishment of the Central Organization for a Durable Peace at The Hague, 1915

When the war broke out in 1914, the governments and parliaments of the various countries had already begun to prepare for a third Hague Peace

Conference, tentatively scheduled for 1915. The outbreak of the Great War temporarily interrupted the movement toward the peaceful settlement of disputes. Many of the rules laid down in The Hague Conventions were violated in World War I. For example, the German invasion of Belgium was a violation of Convention (III) of 1907, which states that hostilities must not commence without explicit warning. Poison gas was introduced and used by all major belligerents throughout the war, in violation of the Declaration (IV, 2) of 1899 and Convention (IV) of 1907, which explicitly forbade the use of "poison or poisoned weapons."[37]

Despite the postponement of a third Hague Peace Conference, peace-minded individuals and leaders of thought continued to seek ways to bring the conflict to a speedy conclusion and to generate ideas to secure a just and lasting peace. Initial impetus for the creation of a body to coordinate activities on a temporary basis was provided by the Dutch peace societies.

Dedicated to promoting the idea of arbitration and preventing war, the Dutch peace groups merged in October 1914 and formed the *Nederlandsche Anti-Oorlog Raad* (Netherlands Anti-War Council, N.A.O.R.), an organization in which all peace groups were represented, including members from all political parties. This new organization was to be temporary in character and to last only until the end of the war. Its aim was "the securing of a peace that will not have in it the germs of a future war."[38] The approach adopted by the group secured the cooperation of all classes—workers and socialists as well as different Christian denominations and members of the middle class.[39] Working in collaboration with the Swiss Committee for the Study of a Durable Peace, the Netherlands Anti-War Council (N.A.O.R.) circulated a manifesto, which included a "Minimum Program" for a durable peace, and invited all those in other countries who agreed with its contents to unite in plans for "the peace which is bound to come, and which should not find us unprepared."[40]

The purpose of the Minimum Program was to focus discussion on the means for guaranteeing a durable peace at the conclusion of the war. In addition to envisaging the establishment of a permanent peace organization concerned with the settlement of all disputes between states, and which would have periodic meetings, the Program listed issues, requiring careful consideration, including the peaceful regulation of international relations, the setting of frontiers, political imperialism and expansion as the causes of conflict and their impact on trade, and the like. It also called for a careful study of these issues at a national level with a view to formulating specific proposals to be brought before a third Hague Peace Conference.[41]

Creation of the Central Organization for a Durable Peace at The Hague

The response to the Manifesto from peace groups in other countries was so encouraging that the Netherlands Anti-War Council decided to convene an international meeting at The Hague in April 1915 to discuss the basis of a durable peace. It was from this meeting that the Central Organization for a Durable Peace at The Hague was created.

Delegates from forty countries, including all the belligerent states, were invited to participate in the April 1915 meeting. Given the challenges involved in obtaining passports, and travel during wartime, only thirty delegates from ten countries were able to attend. Five neutral countries were represented (the United States, Norway, Holland, Sweden, and Switzerland). And five belligerent countries were represented (Germany, Great Britain, Belgium, Austria, and Hungary).[42] Those who attended The Hague gathering were persons of distinction. They included nine members of parliament; leading academics in the fields of economics, education, history, international law, philosophy, and medicine; and lawyers, intellectuals, and humanitarians dedicated to exploring new forms of international organization. Many of the delegates were later involved in the formulation of the League of Nations.[43]

Given the political sensitivity of discussing peace during wartime and involving the participation of delegates from the contending parties in the discussions, the initial deliberations of the delegates were conducted in private. At the conclusion of the meeting, the *New York Times* announced the formation of the Central Committee for the Organization of a Durable Peace with the headline, "Mysterious Hague Meeting, Not to End Present War, but to Prevent Future Ones." Dated April 12, 1915, the *Times* article refers to delegates from a number of countries engaging in "private discussion of peace," the "drafting of a program for action," and provides the following "short record of the work of the conference":

> The object of the meeting was not to suggest steps to bring the war to an end, but to consider by what principles the future peace of the world would best be guaranteed. After a full discussion a minimum program was unanimously adopted.
>
> The action to be initiated in the different countries will ultimately be supplemented by an international propaganda. A central committee for a durable peace has been created as a link between the national organizations. The committee of the Dutch anti-war council, supplemented by members from other countries, will serve as the executive. Mrs. Fanny F. Andrews of Boston was the American delegate.[44]

The newly created body, the Central Organization for a Durable Peace, focused its immediate attention on initiating planning and laying the basis of "the new world order which must come after the present war." Conscious of the formidable task confronting the peacemakers—"they will be charged with nothing less than a general reorganization of international procedure"—the Organization identified the following priority for action: "The moment calls for full and free discussion, for in no other way can wise conclusions be reached. The obligation of the present, then, is to formulate and to promulgate the plans for a new departure in international procedure. We may mold history tomorrow if we can mold opinion today."[45]

The deliberations of the April 1915 meeting of the Central Organization were concerned primarily with elaborating the points contained in the Minimum Program. According to Doty, "It was agreed that each resolution in the program should embody a principle and that an attempt should be made in formulating the principle to unite the moderate elements in the opposing camps and all those who saw the war as the result of grave defects in the international organization."[46] The Minimum Program was offered to the world "as a foundation for common action."[47] Details of the Minimum Program included the following:

1. No annexation or transfer of territory shall be made contrary to the interests and wishes of the population concerned. Where possible their consent shall be obtained by plebiscite or otherwise.

The States shall guarantee to the various nationalities, included in their boundaries, equality before the law, religious liberty and the free use of their native languages.

2. The States shall agree to introduce in their colonies, protectorates and spheres of influence, liberty of commerce, or at least equal treatment for all nations.

3. The work of The Hague Conferences with a view to the peaceful organization of the Society of Nations shall be developed.

The Hague Conference shall be given a permanent organization and meet at regular intervals.

The States shall agree to submit all their disputes to peaceful settlement. For this purpose there shall be created, in addition to the existent Hague Court of Arbitration, (a) a permanent Court of International Justice, (b) a permanent international Council of Investigation and Conciliation. The States shall bind themselves to take concerted action, diplomatic, economic or military, in case any State should resort to military measures instead of submitting the dispute to judicial decision or to the mediation of the Council of Investigation and Conciliation.

4. The States shall agree to reduce their armaments. In order to facilitate the reduction of naval armaments, the right of capture shall be abolished and the freedom of the seas assured.

5. Foreign policy shall be under the effective control of the parliaments of the respective nations.

Secret treaties shall be void.[48]

The aim of the Central Organization for a Durable Peace was to encourage the formation of national groups in all countries. These groups would make a technical study of the proposals laid down in the Minimum Program. Nine research committees, representing the nine points of the Minimum Program, were organized. The importance of these study groups extended beyond the resolution of technical issues. They were, in addition, a vital means of galvanizing international support for the efforts of the Central Organization's approach to ensuring a broad, principled-based settlement at the end of the war. Andrews sets out the vision as follows: "The work of the Central Organization for a Durable Peace may be described as a simultaneous world study to prepare for action at the supreme moment of the world's history which we shall witness after the war. This moment will call for high statesmanship—a statesmanship freed from bias, resting its action on legal principles, and motived by the desire to establish the eternal laws of justice and humanity."[49]

The Central Organization recognized the necessity of organizing peace, "if it is to be durable"[50] and believed this could be achieved if the work of The Hague Peace Conferences were to be developed and made permanent, and if the provisions encouraging Governments to agree to submit differences to arbitration rather than having recourse to war were to be strengthened. To this end, the conference agreed to create a permanent bureau at The Hague charged with the functions of calling the future international congress and fixing the date. This central body was to be a rallying point for peace programs of all countries, for as the war went on, it was anticipated that peace activities in the belligerent nations were likely to become more difficult.

The April 1915 meeting of the Central Organization concluded after four days. Before adjourning, a small Executive Committee, based in Holland, was set up to conduct the affairs of the Organization, including the appointment of study groups and the printing and distribution of the Manifesto and the Minimum Program. The distribution of the principles underlying the Minimum Program was critical to winning widespread support for achieving an enduring peace, rather than a mere armistice. In the longer term, it was hoped that by making a worldwide appeal to the mass of humankind and by securing the support of as many followers as possible to the principles laid down in the Manifesto and Minimum Program—at a favorable moment or by the end of the war—it might be possible to convene an international congress with representatives from all nations to endorse and elaborate the Minimum Program.

The Central Organization for a Durable Peace was aware that "the stability of peace will never be maintained by measures of international order alone."[51] Echoing this view, G. Lowes Dickinson wrote, "There must be a drastic change, first in the spirit animating nations, and then, as a consequence, in institutions, if civilization is to be saved from the menace with which it is threatened. Such changes must derive their impulse not from Governments and Foreign Offices, but from the people."[52]

Regarding the outcome of the study groups, the Minimum Program was a set of principles rather than a working program. It was an attempt to formulate practical ideals of which the world was in need and which possibly might be realized with the hope that in due course, a series of conventions or treaties might be drafted that would show how these principles might be put into effect. Unfortunately, the circumstances of the war prevented the meeting of international conferences to discuss and elaborate on the Minimum Program. While much work was done, the latter part of the Central Committee's program could never be adequately carried out. As a result, there was no complete documentation of the Minimum Program to present to the Peace Conference at Paris that might have made the Minimum Program an important document in the formation of the League of Nations.[53]

Assessing the uniqueness of this gathering and its contribution to the discourse on peace, Doty observed, "[T]he Central Organization was the only

71

international body which during the war brought together men prominent in political life in both the belligerent and neutral countries and which managed to agree on a program that was accepted by all. Its work is noteworthy as indicating what the highest intelligences of that day thought were the most urgent reforms needed and what they believed could be achieved."[54]

While the third Hague Peace Conference, planned for 1915, was usurped by the First World War, four years of trench warfare hardened public opinion, and some of the Conference's ideals were institutionalized in a Permanent Meeting of the League of Nations in Switzerland. In The Hague the ideals found expression in the construction of the world-famous Peace Palace, financed by Andrew Carnegie, and officially opened in 1913 on the eve of the First World War. Home to the Permanent Court of Arbitration, it welcomed the Permanent Court of International Justice (under the League of Nations) in 1922 and is now the seat of its successor, the International Court of Justice, the principal judicial organ of the United Nations.

The Women's International League for Peace and Freedom

A second historic meeting took place in The Hague in April 1915. On the evening of April 27, 1915, two weeks after the meeting of the Central Organization, the Women's International League for Peace and Freedom met at The Hague. The Women's International League was the only body, apart from the Central Organization for a Durable Peace, to hold an international congress during the war and to formulate a program. Between twelve hundred and two thousand women representing twelve nations journeyed to The Netherlands to plead for peace at The Hague. The event was instigated by Dr. Aletta Jacobs (1854–1929), a Dutch physician and the best-known woman reformer in her country.[55]

The four-day peace congress was attended by women from Holland, England, Germany, Austria, Hungary, the northern European neutral countries, and the United States of America. The American delegation of forty-seven accomplished American women, led by Jane Addams (1860–1935), president of the recently formed Women's Peace Party (WPP),[56] made a significant contribution to the gathering.[57]

The agenda of the women's peace congress focused on prospects for mediation and principles for international reform. The congress endorsed the setting up of a neutral conference to engage in continuous mediation, serve as a clearing house for peace feelers, and encourage both the Allies and the Central Powers to consider peace discussions. The congress also passed resolutions identifying underlying causes of war and advancing prescriptive remedies for the postwar world. These resolutions were very similar to the Minimum Program outlined by the Program of the Central Organization for a Durable Peace. Both programs embodied principles that were circulating among many nations, and both organizations considered the social and economic aspects of peace, stood for national determination and the rights of minorities, and sought to promote international cooperation. There were, however, differences in emphasis for each program. For example, unlike the Central Organization, the Women's International League was more focused on bringing the war to a speedy end by a negotiated peace and was not content with merely formulating a program for a durable peace in the future. Consequently, the Women's International League opted to pursue an independent course of action. Their delegates voted to send women envoys to present the resolutions to the governments in Europe and the United States. Patterson describes the outcome of the latter initiative: "Despite serious logistical difficulties, the women managed to visit nearly all the warring and neutral European nations (except neutral Spain and Portugal, the smaller countries in southeastern Europe, and the Ottoman Empire), and were respectfully received by the prime ministers and foreign ministers as well as Pope Benedict XV (1854–1922). The political leaders of neutral Holland and Sweden showed considerable interest in mediation."[58]

The activities of the Women's International League contributed greatly to the movement toward peace. Women reformers were already well-connected internationally before the war from their participation in biennial meetings of the International Woman Suffrage Alliance (IWSA), an association founded in the first years of the century and that, by 1914, had become a loose affiliation of over twenty national suffrage groups. In 1913, the IWSA held its International Congress in Budapest, Hungary. Dr. Susan I. Moody, a physician and an American Bahá'í who resided in Iran, sent a telegraph to the Congress greeting those in attendance on behalf of the Bahá'í women in Iran. In her presidential opening remarks, the international president of the congress, an American by the name of Mrs. Carrie C. Catt, mentioned receiving the telegraph. Carrie Catt asked Moody to provide her with some information about the Bahá'í women in Iran so that she could include it in a piece that she was working on at the time. Moody wrote to 'Abdu'l-Bahá about Catt's request. He replied with a letter in which He listed the names of a number of Iranian Bahá'í women, characterizing them as knowledgeable, eloquent in speech and oratory, and accomplished in writing poetry and ballads. He also described the courage, firmness, and steadfastness of a number of Bahá'í women that were murdered in the province of Yazd, Iran, located some 170 miles southeast of Isfahan, Iran.[59]

The IWSA provided a forum for the exploration of "the transnational dimensions of the relationship between feminist issues, on the one hand, and militarism and war, on the other." With the outbreak of the war, many of its internationalist-oriented members actively campaigned for neutral mediation of the conflict. The transforming event in this movement took place in April 1915, when women from twelve nations arrived in The Hague to plead for peace.[60]

The Postwar Era

Following the cessation of hostilities in 1918, peace activists of the Great War era continued to work energetically for peace. Indeed, peace movements exerted an important influence in the politics and diplomacy of the 1920s and 1930s. The pervasive popular disillusionment with the Great War, together with growing fears of another world war, stimulated a strong, renewed interest in peace.

Dissolution of the Central Organization for a Durable Peace at The Hague

With the signing of the Treaty of Versailles in Paris in 1919, the Central Organization for a Durable Peace largely ceased its activities. Writing on this subject, Doty observed that "after 1919 one rarely finds the name of the Central Organization mentioned." Exploring "[T]he neglect, the silence and the resistance of the Allies to the work of the Hague," she identified as the "chief reason" the fact that "the Central Organization based its proposals on the Hague Conferences [of 1899 and 1907], . . . and that as soon as the idea of a League of Nations was adopted the Hague Conferences were dropped into the background and that the Central Organization based as it was on the Hague Conferences met a similar fate."[61]

Doty cited at length the views of German pacifist and international legal scholar, Professor Hans Wehberg (1885–1962). Wehberg was a participant in both the 1899 and 1907 Hague Peace Conferences and, along with Walther Schücking, is regarded as the founder of the pacifist theory of international law.[62] Wehberg offered two reasons why, during the drafting of the Covenant of the League of Nations, The Hague Peace Conferences were ignored. First, Wehberg believed that the longer the war lasted, the stronger the feeling grew that The Hague Conferences were ineffectual in maintaining peace. The chief criticisms were that The Hague conventions had not made arbitration obligatory and that unanimity was required in all decisions. "That," Wehberg stated, "is one of the reasons for the manifest opposition to the continuance of the work of the Hague." Little by little, this view gained traction and resulted in the demand for a new form of organization and thus the idea of a League of Nations was born, and the work of The Hague sunk into the background.[63]

While it is true that some delegates proposed a third Hague Conference be called, there was strong disagreement concerning who should participate in the gathering. A third Hague Conference would have been more inclusive and would have involved the participation of the Central Powers, and the Allies were determined this should not happen. According to Wehberg, this was the second reason for neglecting The Hague.[64]

The Central Organization, similar to all other organizations that had German members, was regarded with suspicion. As the war progressed, there arose a distrust among the belligerents about the work of the Central Organization for a Durable Peace. In Germany, for example, the Organization was accused of being anti-German, while in England it had the reputation of being pro-German. In her writings, Jane Addams spoke of the great antagonism that arose to all pacifists as being pro-German after the United States entered the war, and she noted that even the programs of the Central Organization were looked upon with suspicion.

Given the lack of direct evidence and the scarcity of articles on its work, Doty believed it was difficult to assess what influence the Central Organization had on public opinion. The organization undoubtedly had an influence through men and women who endorsed its program and who joined the organization's International Council. Many of its members were deeply committed to its Minimum Program and later were involved in the League of Nations.[65] Elaborating on this theme, Doty observed that ". . . in spite of the silence in which America's entry into the war buried the work of the . . . Central Organization their principles continued to have their influence on many people including Wilson. For at the conclusion of the war it was these same principles that Wilson advocated at the peace table when he fought to have incorporated in the Covenant, territorial integrity, the right of self-determination, the rights of minorities, the desirability of liberty of commerce, some sort of democratic control of foreign policy, the reduction of armaments and the abolition of secret treaties."[66] Writing in 1945, Doty observed, "In the final summing up of the work of the Central Organization one is impressed with the fact that 30 years ago a group of men and women saw so clearly the fundamental issues at stake in creating a Society of Nations."[67]

The Unfinished Business

When the second Hague Peace Conference ended in 1907, America's Secretary of State, Elihu Root, instructed the American delegate, Joseph Choate, to obtain a resolution calling for a third conference to be held within another seven to eight years. Undismayed by the conference's minimal results, Root understood that successive failures were necessary for success. He responded to the criticism of disappointed peace activists by offering a different perspective: The measure of the success of each International Conference was not merely what it had accomplished but also what it had begun and accelerated.[68]

The guns of August 1914 rudely interfered with the implementation of this resolution. The third Conference envisioned by Secretary Root was eventually held in The Hague in May 1999, at the initiative of the Russian and Dutch governments. It was not a treaty-making conference like the first two, but a centennial commemoration on the theme "The Peaceful Settlement of Disputes: Prospects for the Twenty-First Century." Inspired by The Hague Peace Conferences, a large segment of civil society linked by common interests and collective activity, seized the opportunity to hold its own conference on the theme, "The Hague Appeal for Peace 1999."[69]

The Hague Appeal was inspired by the past work of peace activists, including Bertha von Suttner, who is reported to have said, "Whatever is expressed by the Peace Movement is not a dream by people far removed from reality; rather it is civilization's drive to sustain itself."[70] It might be said that the third Hague Peace Conference

sent a clear message to the world's policy makers on issues with which they failed to address in the first two rounds: How to eliminate the causes of war; including racism, colonialism, poverty and other human rights violations, the limitation of arsenals to a reasonable level for territorial defense, the elimination of all weapons of mass destruction including nuclear ones, the establishment and utilization of conflict resolution mechanisms (as an interim measure on the way to abolish war), improvements in humanitarian law, and most importantly, the creation of a culture of peace for the world's war-oppressed people.[71]

5 / 'Abdu'l-Bahá's Contribution to Peace

Each of the divine Educators can well be regarded as an "All-Knowing Physician" Who has placed "His finger on the pulse of mankind." Developing the medical analogy, Bahá'u'lláh describes how the skilled physician, "perceiveth the disease, and prescribeth, in His unerring wisdom, the remedy." And commenting on the inevitability of change and the uniqueness of each new era, He observes that as "Every age hath its own problem, and every soul its particular aspiration. The remedy the world needeth in its present-day afflictions can never be the same as that which a subsequent age may require." Underlining this important notion, Bahá'u'lláh advises humanity to be "concerned with the needs of the age ye live in, and center your deliberations on its exigencies and requirements."[1]

The mission of the Faith of Bahá'u'lláh is to usher in an age of peace and world unity. The achievement of this transformative undertaking involves not only a profound change in human values—the emergence of a deep and abiding appreciation of the oneness and wholeness of humankind—but also the creation of global institutions necessary for the establishment of just and unified relationships between the peoples and nations of the world. War must be eliminated and universal peace firmly established.

A World Without War

Bahá'u'lláh passed away in 'Akká in 1892. In His Book of the Covenant (His will and testament), He appointed 'Abdu'l-Bahá as His successor and head of the Bahá'í Faith. Throughout His life, 'Abdu'l-Bahá played a vital role in elucidating the teachings of the Bahá'í Faith and fostering the development of embryonic Bahá'í communities to demonstrate the transformative impact of the teachings on individual and social life. His whole being was devoted to the promotion of universal peace. He was an astute observer of world events, was keenly aware of the challenges of contemporary life, and was tireless in engaging in activities to ameliorate the human condition.

Underlining Bahá'u'lláh's advice to humanity—to be "concerned with the needs of the age ye live in, and center your deliberations on its exigencies and requirements,"[2] 'Abdu'l-Bahá calls attention to the fact that "In every century a particular and central theme is, in accordance with the requirements of that century, confirmed by God." He identifies the current theme: "In this illumined age that which is confirmed is the oneness of the world of humanity," and stresses its importance, affirming: "Without such unity, rest and comfort, peace and universal reconciliation are unachievable."[3]

This chapter and the one that follows explore the contributions of 'Abdu'l-Bahá to peace. Three main topics are discussed. The first is 'Abdu'l-Bahá's involvement in the discourses of peace during His travels to the West in 1911–1913, including His participation in the Lake Mohonk Peace gathering in upstate New York in 1912. The second is the important role of the Tablets of the Divine Plan, fourteen letters He addressed to His followers in North America in 1916–1917, in furthering the peace process. Written during the darkest period of the First World War these remarkable letters offered an alternative vision of human society, laid out strategies and guiding principles for achieving a peaceful world, and assigned certain responsibilities for spreading the values of peace throughout the globe. A third subject, which is taken up in the following chapter, concerns the historic Tablets 'Abdu'l-Bahá wrote to the Executive Committee of the Central Organization for a Durable

Peace at The Hague in 1919–1920 and His appointment of a delegation of two Iranian Baháʼís to meet with this organization on His behalf.

'Abdu'l-Bahá: the Champion for Peace

Exiled as a nine-year-old child, with His Father and members of His family, from Iran in 1853, 'Abdu'l-Bahá remained a religious prisoner of the Ottoman Empire in ʻAkká until 1908, when the Young Turk Revolution resulted in the overthrow of the regime of Ottoman Sultan 'Abdu'l Ḥámid II. The revolution restored the 1876 Ottoman Constitution, establishing a constitutional government that led to the release of all religious and political prisoners held under the old government. After over forty years in exile, 'Abdu'l-Bahá was freed from prison. He was sixty-four years old.

With His freedom in hand, 'Abdu'l-Bahá moved to the nearby port city of Haifa in pre-mandatory Palestine. He spent the next several years attending to important matters that related to the development of the Baháʼí Faith. In the summer of 1911, although in frail health after more than half a century in exile, He set out on a journey that lasted until December 1913.

His travels took him from Haifa to several locations in Egypt, then to Europe, the United Kingdom, the United States, and Canada. The purpose of the trip was to foster the development of the Baháʼí Faith in the West and to familiarize the public with its spiritual and social principles applicable to the new age that was unfolding before humanity. Betterment of humanity's spiritual and material condition, progress, happiness, kindness, tranquility, trust, fellowship, unity, justice, oneness, and beauty were just some of the themes that 'Abdu'l-Bahá spoke about on His travels in Egypt and in the Western hemisphere. In His speeches and conversations with so many different people throughout His journey, 'Abdu'l-Bahá introduced the Faith's new ideas, explained its realistic and practical principles, and demonstrated the relevance of these principles to the efforts of the individual, society, and social institutions in their efforts to establish peace.

The scope of His travels was vast and widespread. Among the many places He visited during His voyage were Cairo, Thonon-les Bains, France; Paris, London, Oxford, Edinburgh, Bristol, Stuttgart, Budapest, and Vienna. In North America, He traveled to New York City, Boston, Worcester, Washington, DC, Chicago, Cleveland, Pittsburgh, Brooklyn, Philadelphia, West Englewood, Jersey City, Cambridge, Buffalo, Minneapolis/St. Paul, Omaha, Denver, Salt Lake City, San Francisco, Oakland, Palo Alto, Berkeley, Pasadena, Los Angeles, Sacramento, Cincinnati, Baltimore, and Montreal.

He spoke at a number of prestigious universities, including Howard University, Columbia University, Stanford University, and Oxford University. He gave talks at settlement houses; conferences; and churches, including Baptist, Unity, Congregational, Catholic, and Universalist. He addressed audiences at synagogues, at women's organizations, at the Theosophical Society, at missions for the very poor, at the fourth annual conference of the National Association for the Advancement of the Colored People, at peace societies, and at others. He met with ministers, ambassadors, religious leaders, suffragettes, students, the poor, university presidents, government officials, business leaders, inventors, scientists, and members of the growing Bahá'í community in the West. Throughout His travels, 'Abdu'l-Bahá presented the Bahá'í teachings and always concentrated on how their application advances human progress, both spiritual and material. He also spoke extensively about the process by which peace can be established in the world, and He examined the obstacles that had prevented humanity from achieving peace.

In a speech delivered in 1912 to an audience gathered at Hotel Sacramento in Oakland, California, 'Abdu'l-Bahá referred to the contents of letters that His Father, Bahá'u'lláh, had addressed to the leaders of the world in the 1860s and 1870s, that focused on Bahá'u'lláh's principle for the elimination of all forms of prejudice as a prerequisite to the establishment of peace. He pointed out that as long as religious, racial, political, national, and sectarian prejudice "continues to exist among mankind," the realization of peace in the world is not possible.[4] In another talk given earlier in the same year, at the All-Souls Church Lincoln Center in Chicago, He said, "Any movement which brings about peace and agreement in human society is truly a divine movement . . . It is the peace element in religion that blends mankind and makes for unity."[5]

In the South End of Boston at Franklin Square House, whose mission was to provide affordable housing for single women who worked long hours for low wages, 'Abdu'l-Bahá told the gathering, "Strive that the ideal of international peace may become realized through the efforts of womankind, for man is more inclined to war than woman, and a real evidence of woman's superiority will be her service and efficiency in the establishment of universal peace."[6]

At Stanford University, He was introduced by the president of the university, Dr. David Starr Jordan, to two thousand students, faculty, and administrators gathered at the campus' Assembly Hall. 'Abdu'l-Bahá spoke about the importance of those individuals who devote their time to science and knowledge. He said, "the noblest center is a center wherein the sciences and arts are taught and studied. Science ever tends to the illumination of the world of humanity."[7] Toward the conclusion of the talk, He summoned His audience to champion the cause of peace and "human upliftment" through the application of scientific knowledge, and spiritual principles:

> We are all human. . . . and all come from [one origin]. Why, then, all these fallacious national and racial distinctions? These boundary lines and artificial barriers have been created by despots and conquerors who sought to attain dominion over mankind . . . As a rule they themselves enjoyed luxuries in palaces, surrounded by conditions of ease and affluence, while armies and soldiers, civilians and tiller of the soil fought and died at their command upon the field of battle, shedding their innocent blood for a delusion such as "we are Germans," "our enemies are French," etc., when, in reality, all are humankind.[8]

And, addressing the academic assembly, He stated, "I supplicate God that He may confirm and assist you, that each one of you may become a professor emeritus in the world of scientific knowledge, a faithful standard-bearer of peace and bonds of agreement between the hearts of men."[9]

In September 1912, at the St. James Methodist Church in Montreal, 'Abdu'l-Bahá identified war as the biggest calamity facing the world. In particular, He called attention to the troubling developments in arms proliferation among the empires of the European continent and the danger that this expansion posed for the outbreak of war. He said, "The greatest catastrophe in the world of humanity today is war. Europe is a storehouse of explosives awaiting a spark. All the European nations are on edge, and a single flame will set on fire the whole of the continent."[10]

While traveling in Canada, many newspapers covered His trip. The front-page headline of *The Montreal Daily Star* on August 31, 1912 read, "APOSTLE OF PEACE HERE PREDICTS AN APPALLING WAR IN THE OLD WORLD." 'Abdu'l-Bahá was quoted as having said, "All Europe is an armed camp. These warlike preparations will necessarily culminate in a great war. The very armaments themselves are productive of war. This great arsenal must go ablaze. There is nothing of the nature of prophecy about such a view," said 'Abdu'l-Bahá; "it is based on reasoning solely."[11]

Given His astute observations about the state of the world and His concerns about the threat of war, it is not surprising that throughout His long journey in the West, He chose to speak to His audiences about the approaching catastrophe. He was aware that leaders in Europe were anxious about the arms race and that each empire was busily engaged in developing new and larger weapons of war.

It is important to note, however, that it was not 'Abdu'l-Bahá's aim nor the primary intention of His talks to focus only on the barbarism and horrors of war. Rather, He sought to speak about peace and the possibility of its attainment in the fast-changing and unfolding world that was being fashioned under the shadow of the old. Indeed, peace was the prominent theme throughout 'Abdu'l-Bahá's talks. His objective was to communicate His Father's all-inclusive, comprehensive teachings about how to shape and form a new world free from the prejudices that fuel violence and conflict.

'Abdu'l-Bahá understood the challenges involved in achieving peace. His approach was realistic. He did not hesitate to call attention to the demanding work entailed in peacemaking or to the difficult task of building a solid foundation for the spread of moral and spiritual principles and values. "Today the benefits of universal peace," He wrote, "are recognized amongst the people, and likewise the harmful effects of war are clear and manifest to all. But in this matter, knowledge alone is far from sufficient: A power of implementation is needed to establish it throughout the world."[12] He went on to explain that "the power of implementation in this great endeavor is the penetrating influence of the Word of God and the confirmations of the Holy Spirit."[13]

In relation to the theme of "the power of implementation," it is interesting to note that many years earlier, in a letter that He had written anonymously in 1875 at the request of His Father, 'Abdu'l-Bahá explained the role of spiritual knowledge in the transformation of human actions. His letter, subsequently published under the title *The Secret of Divine Civilization*,[14] was addressed to the people of Iran. It outlined the challenge of modernity including, among its features, "constitutional and democratic government, the rule of law, universal education, the protection of human rights, economic development, religious tolerance, the promotion of useful sciences and technologies and programmes of public welfare."[15] In this letter, 'Abdu'l-Bahá stated that a purely material civilization, devoid of spiritual values and "unsupported by a genuine civilization of character," is incapable of bringing "about the peace and well-being of the people." "Does it not, rather," He continued, "connote the destruction of man's estate and pull down the pillars of happiness and peace?"[16] He went on to observe:

There are some who imagine that an innate sense of human dignity will prevent man from committing evil actions and insure his spiritual and material perfection. That is, that an individual who is characterized with natural intelligence, high resolve, and a driving zeal, will, without any consideration for the severe punishment consequent on evil acts, or for the great rewards of righteousness, instinctively refrain from inflicting harm on his fellow men and will hunger and thirst to do good. And yet, if we ponder the lessons of history it will become evident that this very sense of honor and dignity is itself one of the bounties deriving from the instructions of the Prophets of God.[17]

Contact with Leaders of Thought

Examination of the record of 'Abdu'l-Bahá's travels illustrates His ability to communicate at a deep level with people of different cultures and backgrounds. He was not held back by considerations of race, of class, of gender or of religious belief: "Tirelessly, He expounded the teachings in every social space: in homes and mission halls, churches and synagogues, parks and public squares, railway carriages and ocean liners, clubs and societies, schools and universities. . . . To all without distinction—officials, scientists, workers, children, parents, exiles, activists, clerics, skeptics—He imparted love, wisdom, comfort, whatever the particular need."[18]

He invited all those with whom He came in contact to examine the relevance of the teachings of Bahá'u'lláh to the needs of the society in which they lived. He was "Uncompromising in defence of the truth, yet infinitely gentle in manner," and "He brought the universal divine principles to bear on the exigencies of the age."[19]

He sought out people who were advocates of peace and eager to find means to prevent war. Arriving in Egypt in 1910, one year before His departure for Europe, 'Abdu'l-Bahá met with intellectuals, peace activists, and religious leaders—including a number of British Quakers—and He was interviewed by representatives of the Egyptian and European press, who were curious about His ideas and perspective on the state of the world.

Throughout His travels, and indeed throughout His life, 'Abdu'l-Bahá made the promotion of the discussion of peace a high priority. For example, in England, 'Abdu'l-Bahá spoke about peace and engaged with suffragettes and peacemakers; in Paris, He responded to questions from a journalist about the failure of the recent (1907) Hague Conference to bring about international peace; and, in Vienna, He received Baroness von Suttner, a well-known worker for the cause of peace who, in her pursuit of peace, was reported to have asserted, "Whatever is expressed by the Peace Movement is not a dream by people far removed from reality; rather it is civilization's drive to sustain itself."[20]

In the United States, 'Abdu'l-Bahá spoke before peace societies; He again met up with Bertha von Suttner in the home of a prominent Bahá'í, Corinne True; and He was invited to speak at Hull House, in Chicago, by reformer and peace activist, Jane Addams.[21] He had contact with Andrew Carnegie,[22] the renowned philanthropist who endowed the Peace Palace at The Hague, and, in a Tablet written in 1915, praised Carnegie's activities in promoting "peace and the principle of the unification of mankind and the establishment of universal peace."[23]

Lake Mohonk Peace Conference

From the beginning, 'Abdu'l-Bahá took a keen interest in efforts to bring into existence a new international order. For example, His early public references in North America concerning the purpose of His visit placed particular emphasis on the invitation He received from the organizing committee of the Lake Mohonk Peace Conference requesting Him to address the international conference. Indeed, one of the highlights of 'Abdu'l-Bahá's visit to North America was His participation at the eighteenth Lake Mohonk Peace Conference on International Arbitration, which was held from May 15 to 17, 1912.

The gatherings at Lake Mohonk were the results of the initiative of two Quaker brothers, Albert K. and Daniel Smiley. The first Conference on International Arbitration, which had as its aim "creating and directing public sentiment in favor of international arbitration, arbitration treaties and an international court," was held in 1895.[24]

While in Egypt, 'Abdu'l-Bahá had exchanged correspondence with Mr. Albert Smiley, founder and president of the conference, and also with Harry Clinton Phillips, the conference's secretary. As a result, in November 1911, 'Abdu'l-Bahá had been invited to be the featured speaker at the 18th Annual Conference, and He had scheduled His visit to the United States to include this important event.[25]

The 1912 conference at Lake Mohonk was attended by over 180 prominent people from various fields, such as judges, presidents of universities and chambers of commerce, editors of leading newspapers and magazines, diplomats, religious and labor leaders, politicians and future prime ministers, and Nobel prize winners. Newspaper coverage was widespread. Many of the articles included photographs of 'Abdu'l-Bahá and listed the following prominent speakers from abroad: Dr. Christian I. Lange, secretary of the Interparliamentary Union, and Dr. Albert Gobat, director of the International Peace Bureau at Berne, who were slated to discuss the work of their respective organizations; Dr. Otfried Nippold, professor of international law in Berne University, who was to speak on "The Third Hague Conference," the gathering that had tentatively been scheduled to take place in 1915; and 'Abdu'l-Bahá Abbas of Persia, leader of the Bahá'í movement. The American Press Association distributed a picture of the Bahá'í delegation at Lake Mohonk. In addition to 'Abdu'l-Bahá, the photograph included Edward C. Getsinger, Lua Getsinger, Amín Faríd, Aḥmad Sohráb, Mírzá Varqá, Siyyid Assad'u'lláh, and Dr. Ziá Baghdádí. A second portrait of 'Abdu'l-Bahá was released by the Press Association with the caption reading: "'Abdul-Bahá Abbas of Persia, is perhaps the most picturesque figure at the conference on international arbitration being held at Lake Mohonk, N.Y. There are delegates from nearly all nations, and many of those from foreign counties wear their native garb. 'Abdul-Bahá Abbas wears flowing robes, and his long white beard gives him a patriarchal appearance. He is the head of a new religion of peace, and he is making a tour of the world in an effort to unite all churches in the interest of arbitration as a means of settling disputes."[26]

The sessions of the conference were presided over by Nicholas M. Butler, who was then president of Columbia University and president of the Carnegie Endowment for International Peace. 'Abdu'l-Bahá spoke on the evening of first day of the conference. He chose for His subject "The Oneness of the Reality of Humankind." Other speakers at the same session included high-ranking officials from Nicaragua and Argentina; Baron Eduard de Neufville from Germany, member of the German Peace Society and nominated for the Nobel prize in 1913; the editor of the Toronto *Standard*; and the secretary of the American Peace and Arbitration League.[27]

A copy of 'Abdu'l-Bahá's talk is provided in Appendix 1. In preparation for the presentation, the text of His talk was sent from Egypt to the United States in early 1912 and was translated into English by Aḥmad Sohráb. The conference organizers had requested a translation of 'Abdu'l-Bahá's address to be used with the press and to be read after His presentation in Persian.[28]

'Abdu'l-Bahá's speech to the Lake Mohonk gathering focused on the significance of the historical moment and the uniqueness of the twentieth century. He began by referring briefly to causes of the turmoil, conflict, and warfare that had plagued the world in the earlier century, and He highlighted the fact that "At such a time as this, His Holiness, Bahá'u'lláh appeared." 'Abdu'l-Bahá identified the message proclaimed by Bahá'u'lláh, which calls for "the oneness of the world of humanity and the greatest peace," with the means for attaining progress in the twentieth century and beyond. To illustrate His point, He took as an example His country of birth, Persia, and described the impact of Bahá'u'lláh's teachings on those "who accepted His platform and emulated and followed His teachings—whether Christians, Mohammedans, Jews or Zoroastrians." "Among those people," He stated, "the utmost of love and oneness of peace now obtain, for the great teachings of Bahá'u'lláh make for the oneness of the world and for humanity, universal peace and arbitration."[29]

The remainder of 'Abdu'l-Bahá's presentation set out a number of important principles of Bahá'u'lláh that are critical to the attainment of peace. He linked the implementation of these principles to the elimination of prejudices that sustain war: "All the wars which have taken place since the inception of human history have emanated either from religious prejudice, racial prejudice, patriotic prejudice or political greed and interest. As long as these prejudices last, so long will the foundations of humanity tremble. When such prejudices pass away the world will at last find peace." In His concluding remarks, while acknowledging the work of "great philosophers," 'Abdu'l-Bahá also observed that their influence tended to be limited, as they were unable to endow with "ethical education" those who accepted their views. "The greatest peace," He stated, "will not be realized without the power of the Holy Spirit. It is the Holy Spirit of God which insures the safety of humanity, for human thoughts differ, human susceptibilities differ. You cannot make the susceptibilities of all humanity one except through the common channel of the Holy Spirit."[30]

Many in attendance were impressed by 'Abdu'l-Bahá's presentation and came to the platform to thank him, and some embraced him with emotion. *The Washington Herald* reported that he "attracted considerable attention as he delivered, through an interpreter, a message of good will to the audience. The leader of the new born cult (sic) spoke on 'The Oneness of the Reality of Human Kind' and created a profound impression upon his hearers."[31]

'Abdu'l-Bahá also gave two general addresses on the teachings of the Faith and held many private conversations with individuals. His main address and commentaries were featured in the official conference report, and two of His speeches were published in New York newspapers. As His journey across Canada and the United States continued, 'Abdu'l-Bahá had further opportunities to meet a number of the influential people—from universities and peace societies—whom He had first encountered at Lake Mohonk.

On the morning of his departure from the conference, 'Abdu'l-Bahá presented to Mr. Smiley, the president and founder of the Lake Mohonk Conference, a fine Persian carpet as a farewell gift. On receiving the rug, the gentleman was delighted to observe that it was very similar to a rug—much-loved by his wife—that had been destroyed in a fire and that she still sorely missed. Expressing his appreciation, Mr. Smiley exclaimed that his wife would be very happy to receive the new carpet.[32]

'Abdu'l-Bahá spent three productive days at the Lake Mohonk Conference, and though the serene beauty and quiet of Lake Mohonk provided a welcome respite from the bustle of New York City, He was eager to return to the city to take up the next phase of His mission to promote the teachings of Bahá'u'lláh and to continue His work of engaging thinking people in the promotion of peace.

His historic trip to the West came to an end on December 5, 1913, with His return to Haifa. Within a short span of time after His return, World War I exploded on the scene. Within a span of less than five years after the end of the war, the Ottoman Empire collapsed, as did the European empires. The crisis of war and its subsequent destruction and untold human suffering spread to the Middle East and to Haifa. Palestine, which was then an outpost of the crumbling Ottoman Empire, entered the war on the side of Germany, and soon became caught up in the conflict. The region was surrounded by grave dangers. At one time, the threat of the bombardment of Haifa by the Allies was so real that 'Abdu'l-Bahá temporarily evacuated the members of His family and the local Bahá'í community to the inland village of Abú-Sinán.[33]

For the duration of the war, the population of Palestine was subject to severe privations and hardships. The area was isolated, and communication with the rest of the world was, for a period, cut off. Hunger, exacerbated by the neglect of the ruling authorities and the operation of a strict naval blockade, increased the level of suffering. During the war years, 'Abdu'l-Bahá was cut off from communications and correspondence with the outside world. He concentrated His energies on important measures to ease the suffering of the local population, especially those residing in and nearby 'Akká and Haifa.

In anticipation of the outbreak of war, He had purchased land that He farmed, growing grain and other crops. Due to His foresight and management of crop production and the provisions He made for the distribution of grain, He was successful in feeding the poor and partially averting famine among the region's population, who represented the different religious communities in both Haifa and 'Akká. In 1920, the British government officially recognized His humanitarian work and honored him with a knighthood for the services He rendered during the war for the relief of distress and famine.[34]

Promoting the Well-Being of Humanity: The Role of the Tablets of the Divine Plan

As mentioned in chapter 2, the Revelation of Bahá'u'lláh diagnosed the needs of humanity in modern times. The hallmark of His teachings is the pivotal and world-shaping principle of the oneness of humankind, which is destined to give rise to the evolution of a more spiritual and peaceful civilization. In His Tablets to the kings and religious leaders of the earth, Bahá'u'lláh announced the dawning of the long promised age of world peace and brotherhood and asserted that He Himself was the Bearer of the new message and power from God that would transform the prevailing system of antagonism and enmity between people and create the spirit and form of the destined world order. Bahá'u'lláh foresaw and forewarned of the potential for chaos and conflict inherent in the prevailing social and political order, declaring, "Soon will the present-day order be rolled up, and a new one spread out in its stead," and plainly affirmed that the unity of the human race was the essence of His World Order. "The fundamental purpose animating the Faith of God and His Religion," He wrote, "is to safeguard the interests and promote the unity of the human race, and to foster the spirit of love and fellowship amongst men."[35] These historic Tablets have been translated into English and published in a volume titled *The Summons of the Lord of Hosts*.[36]

Bahá'u'lláh called upon the kings to examine His Cause with fairness and justice. He disclosed to them the uniqueness of the God-given opportunity His call presented to them, to make a significant contribution to the establishment of peace in conformity with the divine vision of the unfolding historical process. He enjoined them to take counsel together, to institute the reign of justice, to compose their differences, and reduce their armaments to end the excessive expenditures that were impoverishing their subjects. To this end, the rulers were instructed to convene a world conference and establish a mechanism for collective security and the maintenance of peace.

The failure of the kings and religious leaders to embrace His redemptive plan for the unification and pacification of the world—the convening of a world conference called for by Bahá'u'lláh to consult together about collective security and the creation of mechanisms and administrative structures to ensure peace—set in motion the forces of change foretold by Bahá'u'lláh. These forces contributed to the collapse of their kingdoms and the decline of ecclesiastical structures, the disintegration of the traditional foundations of society, the erosion of its ancient institutions and values, the prolongation of the period of humanity's suffering. The reluctance of the rulers to accept the opportunity presented to them created a unique opportunity for the masses of humanity to assume responsibility for the eventual fulfillment of Bahá'u'lláh's vision. It also gave impetus to the establishment of Bahá'í administrative structures that were destined to serve as the nucleus and pattern of a new world order.[37]

'Abdu'l-Bahá dedicated His life to furthering the Faith of His Father. During His almost lifelong incarceration and throughout the course of His extended travels in the West, 'Abdu'l-Bahá made frequent appeals to those in authority and to the public at large to examine the teachings enunciated by Bahá'u'lláh. He also foreshadowed the impending chaos, the approaching upheavals, and the universal conflagration that was beginning to impact human society.

'Abdu'l-Bahá was greatly saddened by the failure of the world to respond to the call for universal peace set out in the Writings of Bahá'u'lláh and the urgent appeals He Himself had uttered in His public addresses in the West. Shoghi Effendi writes that "Agony filled His soul at the spectacle of human slaughter precipitated through humanity's failure to respond to the summons He had issued, or to heed the warnings He had given."[38] So critical was the need to alleviate the condition of humanity that 'Abdu'l-Bahá turned to the American Bahá'ís for resolute action and provided them with a long-term strategy for ameliorating the human condition.

As 'Abdu'l-Bahá's physical life drew to a close, He set in motion a strategic plan for ensuring the implementation of Bahá'u'lláh's vision of a peaceful and creative world order. Assessing the spiritual needs and capacities of the peoples of the world, He assigned this task to the American Bahá'í community. The world mission entrusted to the American Bahá'ís was set out in the Tablets of the Divine Plan. Designated as "the chosen trustees and principal executors of 'Abdu'l-Bahá's Divine Plan,"[39] the American Bahá'ís were called upon to assume a preponderating role in taking the message of Bahá'u'lláh to all the countries of the world and for effecting the transformation in values necessary for the emergence of a world order characterized by justice, unity, and peace.

Consisting of fourteen letters, which together form the Tablets of the Divine Plan, these seminal documents constitute the supreme charter for the diffusion of the Bahá'í Faith, fashion in broad outline 'Abdu'l-Bahá's master plan for the spiritual regeneration of the world, and set out prerequisites for the creation of durable peace. He unfolds to the small body of His American followers His conception of their spiritual destiny and invests them with "a mandate to plant the banner of His Father's Faith . . . in all the continents, the countries and islands of the globe."[40]

Timing of the Tablets

The historic Tablets of the Divine Plan were written during the darkest days of World War I, at a time when all means of communication between 'Abdu'l-Bahá in Palestine and the community of His followers around the world were disrupted and, for a period, severed. The individual Tablets were revealed at two separate points in time. The first eight Tablets were written between March 26 and April 22, 1916. The second group was penned between February 2 and March 8, 1917. Their delivery was, however, interrupted and delayed by the war. Nine of the Tablets did not arrive in North America until the cessation of hostilities.[41]

The period in which the Tablets of the Divine Plan were written coincides with the time of most intense suffering occasioned by the war. Commenting on the timing of the revelation and the visionary nature of these Tablets, historian Amin Banani writes, "History records this period as one of awesome bloodletting in Europe. It is truly breathtaking to contemplate the devising of the Divine Strategy for the redemption of the planet in the midst of the din and destruction of the old order. The transforming vision of 'Abdu'l-Bahá spreads before us the plans for the spiritual conquest of the globe."[42]

The first group of Tablets, revealed in 1916, coincided with the beginning of a renewed offensive on the Western front and the commencement of the tremendous bombardments, which characterized the ensuing military encounters and resulted in staggering loss of life on both sides. Examples include the historic battles at Verdun and the Somme.[43] This period also saw the principal naval engagement between the British and German fleets.[44] Despite the brevity of the engagement, the outcome of this battle was highly destructive in the long-term since it gave rise to the strategic use of submarines by the Germans to disrupt all forms of shipping, both military and commercial. As a result, trade and commerce were greatly interrupted, and the suffering of civilian populations dramatically increased. The introduction of unrestricted submarine use in January 1917 threatened all shipping, including vessels from neutral countries. Until the introduction of convoys later in the year, it was estimated that one ship out of every four leaving British ports never came home. According to Taylor, "German submarines forced the entry of the United States into the war." It was after the sinking of American ships by German submarines, that the United States declared war on Germany on April 6, 1917.[45] The final six Tablets, penned between February 2 and March 8, 1917, were written against this backdrop of a travailing world and immediately prior to the entry of the United States into the war.

Significance of the Tablets of the Divine Plan

In the Tablets of the Divine Plan, 'Abdu'l-Bahá takes up the unfinished business of promulgating and implementing the salutary message of peace, justice, and unity contained in the Tablets of Bahá'u'lláh addressed to the kings and ecclesiastical leaders of the world. In light of the failure of the kings and religious leaders, 'Abdu'l-Bahá saw the need to put in place specific provisions to ensure the fulfillment of Bahá'u'lláh's mission of peace and unity. The Tablets of the Divine Plan, therefore, assigned primary responsibility for the task to the North American Bahá'ís—a responsibility progressively shared by the worldwide Bahá'í community, and the Tablets also mandated a structured and orderly approach to the implementation of the work. The mission was so vital it could not be left to chance, to the good will of a few dedicated souls.

Enduring Relevance of the Tablets of the Divine Plan

The Tablets of the Divine Plan captured the mood of the day—the complex fusion of anxiety and despair, the intense desire for an end to conflict, and the emergence of a longing for peace. Addressing this heartfelt yearning, 'Abdu'l-Bahá provided a contrasting and uplifting vision of how the world might be. Stressing the need for urgent action, He called for the dissemination of the unifying teachings of Bahá'u'lláh and suggested immediate practical steps to be taken to respond both to the emerging receptivity and to build a lasting and universal peace, a peace based on recognition of a common humanity and the practice of attitudes and values that promote and sustain peace and conduce to the well-being and maturity of humankind. He writes, ". . . this world-consuming war has set such a conflagration to the hearts that no word can describe it. In all the countries of the world the longing for universal peace is taking possession of men. There is not a soul who does not yearn for concord and peace. A most wonderful state of receptivity is being realized. This is through the consummate wisdom of God, so that capacity may be created, the standard of the oneness of the world of humanity be upraised, and the fundamental of universal peace and the divine principles be promoted in the East and the West."[46]

In another letter, He described the impact of war on humankind and stressed the importance of action:

In short, after this universal war, the people have obtained extraordinary capacity to hearken to the divine teachings, for the wisdom of this war is this: That it may become proven to all that the fire of war is world-consuming, whereas the rays of peace are world-enlightening. One is death, the other is life; this is extinction, that is immortality; one is the most great calamity, the other is the most great bounty; this is darkness, that is light; this is eternal humiliation and that is everlasting glory; one is the destroyer of the foundation of man, the other is the founder of the prosperity of the human race.

Consequently, a number of souls may arise and act in accordance with the aforesaid conditions, and hasten to all parts of the world. . . . Thus in a short space of time, most wonderful results will be produced, the banner of universal peace will be waving on the apex of the world and the lights of the oneness of the world of humanity may illumine the universe.[47]

Written at a critical time in the history of humanity, the Tablets of the Divine Plan resonate with the particular needs of that era, and they reflect the stage of development of the Bahá'í community. Nevertheless, the relevance of the guidance included in these historic letters extends far beyond the years 1916–1917. The global vision articulated in 'Abdu'l-Bahá's Tablets of the Divine Plan not only identified specific action priorities for the immediate expansion of the Bahá'í Faith and the alleviation of human suffering, it also defined pathways to ongoing social transformation and has given direction to ongoing peace-building activities undertaken by the Bahá'ís.

An examination of some of the themes directly associated with peace, included in the Tablets of the Divine Plan, will demonstrate the continuing relevance beyond the years 1916–1917.[48] For example, in one of the Tablets, 'Abdu'l-Bahá makes it clear that the historic mission in which the Bahá'í community is engaged is, at heart, a spiritual enterprise. Underlining this theme, He offers the following comment concerning the historical and transformative role of religion in society:

Consider how the religions of God served the world of humanity! How the religion of Torah became conducive to the glory and honor and progress of the Israelitish nation! How the breaths of the Holy Spirit of His Holiness Christ created affinity and unity between divergent communities and quarreling families! How the sacred power of His Holiness Muḥammad became the means of uniting and harmonizing the contentious tribes and the different clans of Peninsular Arabia—to such an extent that one thousand tribes were welded into one tribe; strife and discord were done away with; all of them unitedly and with one accord strove in advancing the cause of culture and civilization, and thus were freed from the lowest degree of degradation, soaring toward the height of everlasting glory![49]

The work to which the Bahá'ís are called is not confined merely to the expansion of the membership of a faith community. 'Abdu'l-Bahá links the actions of the Bahá'ís and like-minded collaborators in sharing the teachings of the Faith to the transformation of the individual and to laying the foundations for enduring social change, and for a culture of peace.

Implicit in the Tablets of the Divine Plan is recognition that the Bahá'í Faith is a religion of constant change and regards all human beings as having the true purpose of participating in an ever-advancing civilization. The Faith aims to create unity between the diverse elements of humankind, and the concept of change is embedded in the teachings of the Bahá'í Faith. To initiate the process of individual and social transformation, 'Abdu'l-Bahá assigns the following practical tasks to His followers: "In every city and village they must occupy themselves with the diffusion of the divine exhortations and advices, guide the souls and promote the oneness of the world of humanity. They must play the melody of international conciliation with such power that every deaf one may attain hearing, every extinct person may be set aglow, every dead one may obtain new life and every indifferent soul may find ecstasy. It is certain that such will be the consummation."[50]

The task assigned to the members of the Bahá'í community is to create a pattern for future society and thereby lay the foundations for the new civilization destined to emerge with the passage of time. The principle of the oneness of humankind proclaimed in the Revelation of Bahá'u'lláh is the major organizing principle for social action and is critical to the eventual attainment of peace. The achievement of this unity is the aim of all Bahá'í activity. To encourage the systematic practice of this principle, in the Tablets of the Divine Plan, 'Abdu'l-Bahá calls upon the world's inhabitants to free themselves from "all ignorant prejudices" and "to work for the good of all." He exhorts them to engage "in the promulgation of the divine principles so that the oneness of the world of humanity may pitch her canopy in the apex of America and all the nations of the world may follow the divine policy."[51] And He links the infusion of spiritual values into the life of society and its institutions with the achievement of a world-embracing, inclusive, and lasting unity.[52]

The far-reaching transformations envisioned in the Bahá'í Writings are challenging and multifaceted. They include understanding the vision of the oneness of humanity, transforming human values and systems of governance, and creating opportunities for peace to emerge. It is anticipated that the process of change will be evolutionary in nature.

The Tablets of the Divine Plan illustrate some of the consciously planful aspects associated with evolutionary change. For example, the Tablets articulate the vision of a peaceful and united world, where "the mirror of the earth may become the mirror of the Kingdom, reflecting the ideal virtues of heaven."[53] To translate this poetic vision into a concrete plan, 'Abdu'l-Bahá specifies that the teachings of the New Day be promulgated throughout all the nations and islands of the world. To assist the American Bahá'ís to approach this massive task in a systematic manner, He not only lists the countries and island groups by name, but He also specifies the order in which this task is to be completed, and he gives priority to certain cities such as Bahia, Brazil and geographic areas such as Alaska and Panama.[54] Furthermore, He calls for a realistic assessment of the manner in which a particular task is completed, and He stresses the importance of having a systematic approach to the work.[55] Finally, 'Abdu'l-Bahá instills an awareness of the long-term nature of the enterprise by use of the analogy of farming. He calls upon His followers to become "heavenly farmers and scatter pure seeds in the prepared soil," and promises that "Throughout the coming centuries and cycles many harvests will be gathered." He states, "Consider the work of former generations. During the lifetime of Jesus Christ the believing, firm souls were few and numbered, but the heavenly blessings descended so plentifully that in a number of years countless souls entered beneath the shadow of the Gospel."[56]

The Tablets of the Divine Plan articulate a spiritually based approach to change that is realistic, long-term, evolutionary, flexible, and organic. In this chapter we examined 'Abdu'l-Bahá's contribution to peace from the perspective of His lifelong commitment to making known Bahá'u'lláh's teachings both within the Bahá'í community and to the world at large. Focusing first on His travels in the West, we considered His involvement in the current discourses on peace and His participation in such peace activities as the Lake Mohonk Peace Conference in 1912. We then considered the significant contribution of the Tablets of the Divine Plan, fourteen letters addressed to the North American Bahá'ís from 1916 to 1917, as both the source of continuing guidance relevant to laying the foundation for a sustainable peace and as a vehicle for diffusing the values of peace in a systematic, sustained manner. In the following chapter, we take up the subject of two Tablets on peace 'Abdu'l-Bahá wrote, in the aftermath of the First World War, to the Executive Committee of the Central Organization for a Durable Peace at The Hague in 1919–20.

6 / Engaging in the Discourse on Universal Peace

'Abdu'l-Bahá wrote several Tablets to the Executive Committee of the Central Organization for a Durable Peace at The Hague. Such was the importance accorded to this event that 'Abdu'l-Bahá appointed a delegation consisting of two Persian Bahá'ís and instructed them to travel to The Netherlands to deliver the Tablets and to serve as His representatives in meetings with the Organization.

In this chapter, we examine the background to the event, how the Tablets came to be written, and the functions performed by the delegation. As a context for understanding the involvement of the Persian believers, we briefly describe the situation in Iran during World War I and the nature of the initial contact with the Central Organization. We introduce the Persian Bahá'ís who brought to the attention of 'Abdu'l-Bahá the existence of the Organization, and who were subsequently appointed to the delegation. We also describe the meetings of the delegation with the Organization, outline the contents of the Tablets, and the response to the Tablets.

War and Peace in Iran

At the beginning of the nineteenth century, the European presence in Iran was felt primarily in the military and diplomatic spheres. Caught in the middle, Iran was destined to remain a buffer state between the territorial

103

ambitions of Russia and Britain. Nevertheless, the transformative forces for change, often originating in the West, progressively impacted other areas of Iranian life and influenced attitudes about individual and state rights, democracy, forms of political organization, nationalism, and the like.

The First World War had a profound effect on the history of many non-European nations, including Iran. With its vast deposits of oil and its geographic location as a land bridge between Europe and the Indian subcontinent, Iran was one of the major theaters of operation between the Great Powers during the First World War. Contrasting "the dominant Eurocentric approach to historiography regarding this period" with its "specific focus on the trench wars in Western Europe," historian, Touraj Atabaki observes that "in Iranian 20th century historiography, the War is remembered not for major military confrontations, but for economic and political hardships embodied in devastating famine and diseases."[1]

The outbreak of the First World War increased foreign intervention in Iran. Atabaki links the intensification of pressures on the Iranian government—caused by the involvement of foreign powers—with the global shift of industry, armies, and naval units from using coal to using oil fuels. This shift, in turn, led to an increased demand for petroleum products and the subsequent increased strategic significance of west Asia:

Persian oil became not only an economic resource of fundamental importance to British interests worldwide, but also a strategic military asset. Its vast oil deposits and its geographic location at the gates of the Indian subcontinent turned Iran into one of the major theaters of war in west Asia. The outbreak of war increased the geopolitical pressure of the major world powers on Iran, causing the long-lasting rifts in Iranian politics to widen. The occupation of north and south Iran by Russian and British troops prompted the Ottomans to invade western and north-western Iran early in the war. If we add to this list of adversities the subversion of German agents who were also active, especially in the south, we start to get a more complete picture of Iran's position in the war. . . .

The war in Europe reached Iran when the Ottoman Empire joined the Central Powers, making Iran a direct neighbour to combatants from both camps: Russia joined Britain in a fight against the Ottoman Empire, which in turn allied with Germany. For Iranians, the declaration of war in Europe and among its imperial neighbours meant more foreign pressure to take sides in a conflict in which Iran had no national interest.[2]

The Iranian government announced its neutrality on November 1, 1914. Nonetheless, Iran ended up as a battlefield for Russian, Turkish, and British troops. The operation of the First World War on Iran's territory had disastrous effects on the local population. Among the afflictions suffered by the populace were hunger, famine, drought, insecurity caused by armed violence, price inflation, and unemployment.

Requisition and confiscation of foodstuffs by occupying armies to feed their soldiers, combined with a severe drought in 1916 and 1917, resulted in a serious famine. By early February, 1918, the famine spread all over the country. In addition to deaths from starvation, epidemics also killed many people.[3] Atabaki describes the tragic outcome: "The colossal food crisis, plus large numbers of soldiers, refugees and destitute people constantly on the move in search of work and survival, facilitated a deadly combination of pandemics and contagious diseases. Cholera, the plague and typhus spread with terrifying speed across the country, claiming huge numbers of deaths every day. . . . Through the end of the war in Europe, Spanish Influenza also reached Iran."[4] Underlining the devastating impact of World War I on Iran, Atabaki observes: "In the historical memory of the Iranians, as those who had lived in the Ottoman Empire, or in other parts of West Asia, the First

World War is remembered as a period of carnage—not primarily because of combat deaths, of which there were certainly many, but much more because of famines and epidemics that claimed far more victims."[5]

At the end of the war, Russian troops withdrew from Iran, as did the Ottomans, who had been defeated in the four-year conflict. Britain was the remaining dominant foreign power in Iran. The Anglo-Persian Agreement of 1919, which gave drilling rights to the Anglo-Persian Oil Company, was widely viewed as an attempt to establish a British protectorate over Iran. However, it aroused considerable opposition, and the *Majlis* (parliament) refused to approve it. The agreement was already dead when, in February 1921, a coup d'état brought to power Riḍá K̲h̲án, commander of the Cossack Brigade. The shah was deposed on October 31, 1925, and two months later, the *Majlis* vested the monarchy in Riḍá K̲h̲án, who adopted the name *Pahlavi* as his family surname, thus ending the rule of the Qájár dynasty.[6]

The Pursuit of Peace

In relation to the pursuit of peace, it is interesting to note that Iran was an active participant in the Peace Conferences that were held at The Hague in 1899 and 1907. The Iranian government sent two delegates to the 1899 Peace Conference[7] and three to the 1907 Peace Conference.[8] As mentioned in an earlier chapter, the 1899 Peace Conference came at the end of a century whose numerous armed conflicts gave birth to the modern movements for arbitration, peace, and humanitarian law. Commenting on the legacy of the two conferences, legal expert Betsy Baker noted that they had forged "procedural means to allow all participants, regardless of size or actual political or military power, to participate in a formal if not always a substantive way in the process of international negotiation."[9]

While Iranian officials participated in the 1899 and 1907 Peace Conferences at The Hague, the historical record does not include reference to a formal role for Iran in the activities leading to the creation of the Central Organization for a Durable Peace at The Hague in 1915.

Building on the work of the two earlier Hague Peace Conferences, the aim of the third meeting was not to discover ways to bring the war to an immediate conclusion but rather to identify principles on which a durable and lasting future peace could be established. To this end, the preparatory gathering held in The Hague in 1915 drafted a manifesto and a nine-pointed minimum program, which was publicized and distributed throughout the world, and encouraged the formation of national branches of the Central Organization to appoint study groups to prepare detailed proposals for the operationalization of the principles embodied in the minimum program.

It is interesting to note that news of the establishment of the Central Organization for a Durable Peace at The Hague in 1915 appeared in newspapers in Tehran, where its translation into Persian was published, along with information about its mission statement regarding the establishment of peace and the abolition of war.[10] The publication of this article in 1915 in *Ruznameh-Iran*, a newspaper in Tehran, was the event that opened the way to communication—which is described in detail in a section below—between a group of Iranian Bahá'ís and the Executive Committee of the Central Organization for a Durable Peace at The Hague.

By way of a footnote, foreign policy analyst Oliver Bast[11] observed that there was growing recognition by Iranians that the end of the war would bring in its wake the emergence of a new international balance of power. In the first half of 1917, when it seemed possible that the war would end, the Persian government, expecting it would have a role in the future Peace Conference, took concrete measures to prepare for peace. It set up a commission to assess damages incurred as a result of foreign occupation. Immediately after the signing of the armistice, Iran submitted its request for reparations to the three principal defeated powers, in the form of an eight-point memorandum. The memorandum dealt with such issues as the uncontested independence of Persia as a member of the international community; the territorial integrity of Iran; the demand for reparation for damages submitted to the belligerents; economic independence; and a request for aid to undertake a program of reforms for the future development of the country. The Iranian delegation to the Versailles Peace Conference in 1918 was led by the Persian minister of Foreign Affairs, Alí-Kulí Khán (Moshaver ol-Mamalek). Mírzá Alí-Kulí Khán was a Bahá'í who acted as an interpreter for 'Abdu'l-Bahá during His visit to the United States when he acted as Chief Diplomatic Representative and Chargé d'Affaires at the Persian Embassy in Washington, DC.[12]

In 1920, Persia became one of the original members of the League of Nations. When Iran protested the Anglo-Persian Agreement of 1919, the newly formed League ruled in favor of Iran.[13] The failed agreement would have granted to the British supreme power over the military and financial affairs in Iran.[14]

The Bahá'í Faith in Iran

The Bahá'í Faith originated in Iran in the middle of the nineteenth century. Since its inception, the religion is not recognized in Iran. Its Persian-born Prophet-Founder, Bahá'u'lláh, along with thousands of the early Iranian followers, were subjected to attacks and severe persecution from government and clergy. While primarily a spiritual movement, the teachings contain a message of hope, of love, and of practical and spiritual reconstruction; they announce the dawning of the long-promised age of world peace and brotherhood and assert that the power inherent in the new message has the potential to transform the prevailing system of antagonism and enmity among the peoples of the world and to create the spirit and form of the future world order.

In earlier chapters, we considered the teachings of Bahá'u'lláh concerning peace and the necessity of laying the foundations of a just and peaceful society, and we examined Bahá'u'lláh's historic letters to the kings and religious rulers of the world—including the Shah of Persia and the Sultan of Turkey—that called on the leaders to convene a world conference and establish a mechanism for collective security and the maintenance of peace.[15] We also observed how 'Abdu'l-Bahá, inspired by the revelation of His Father, devoted His life to furthering efforts to bring into existence a new international order. He demonstrated His commitment to peace through His wide-ranging Writings and correspondence; His travels in Europe and North America; His contacts with statesmen, academics, peace activists, and humanitarians; His participation in the Lake Mohonk Peace Conference; and His nurturance of embryonic Bahá'í communities dedicated to the practice of spiritual and social Bahá'í values. Such was the priority 'Abdu'l-Bahá accorded to the promotion of peace that He was moved to reveal the Tablets of the Divine Plan.

One of the influential groups in Iranian society who had a keen interest in the pursuit of peace were the members of the Bahá'í community, for whom the ideas of reform were a matter of religious belief. Motivated by their faith, Bahá'ís endeavored to implement the spiritual principles and ideas of their Faith.

Commenting on the nature and relative contributions of the various social, religious and ideological movements to the societal milieu in the early years of the twentieth century, historian Soli Shahvar observes: ". . . the new [Bahá'í] faith . . . put strong emphasis on kindness, education and science, just rule and protection of subjects from oppression and injustice, political quietism, loyalty to the state, and much more. The Bahá'í faith thus became a source of religious, moral and social modernism in Qájár Iran . . ."[16] As to the relative impact Bahá'í reformist thought had in Iran, he offers the following comments:

> it would be reasonable to state, at the very least, that the reformist ideas of the Bahá'í faith played some role in the propagation of reform and modernization in Iran. Thus, towards the end of the nineteenth century, reformist ideas and issues such as opposition to tyranny, the need for justice and order, the advent of modern education, etc., were advocated not only in the works of Iranian secular thinkers and imported Persian newspapers . . . but also in the Writings of Bábí and Bahá'í leaders, who, in many cases, called for even more extreme reformist measures than the non-Bahá'í thinkers (as in the case of the rights of women and minori-

ties). Thus, if not one of the prime sources of reformist ideas in Iran, the Bahá'í faith and community were probably one of the major catalysts for the spread of reform in general, and of educational reform in particular. Certainly, through the practice of their beliefs, the Bahá'ís in Iran, with their broad representation in Iranian society, helped to disseminate such ideas as reform, modernization, science, technology, modern education, etc., which are fundamental to the Bahá'í teachings.[17]

In the section below, we describe the engagement of several Iranian Bahá'ís with the Executive Committee of the Central Organization for a Durable Peace at The Hague, an event that resulted in 'Abdu'l-Bahá's entering into correspondence with the Organization.[18] Much of the material is drawn from an account written by Aḥmad Yazdání, one of the participants involved in these communications.[19] The original short narrative is in Persian and titled *Sharḥ-i-Nuzúl-i-Lawḥ-i-Ṣulḥ-i-Láháy* (*The Account of the Revelation of the Peace Tablet to The Hague*). The document was sent by its author to 'Abdu'l-Bahá's successor, Shoghi Effendi, in 1938, and is held in the International Bahá'í Archives, in Haifa, Israel.

Discourse on Peace

The appearance of an article in *Ruznameh-Iran,* a Teheran newspaper, in 1915—announcing the creation of the Central Organization for a Durable Peace at The Hague and describing its goals and program for peace—motivated several Iranian Bahá'ís to prepare a paper setting out the Bahá'í principles on peace and to send it to the Organization with the suggestion that the group's search for ways to a permanent peace would be facilitated if it sought guidance on the subject from 'Abdu'l-Bahá, the Head of the worldwide Bahá'í community. The Organization responded by submitting, through one of the Iranian Bahá'ís, a letter to 'Abdu'l-Bahá.[20]

On reading the newspaper article about the establishment of the Central Organization for a Durable Peace at The Hague and the statement of its program, Aḥmad Yazdání (1891–1977), a twenty-four year old Bahá'í residing in Tehran, was struck by the similarity of some of the ideas of the Central Organization regarding universal peace and the perspective of the Bahá'í Faith on the subject. Yazdání was well-educated and had intellectual interests. He trained as an engineer and held government positions in Iran until 1949. He was fluent in French and Esperanto, and he was an active member of the Esperanto branch in Tehran. In later life, he served as an elected member of the National Spiritual Assembly of the Bahá'ís of Iran and was appointed to various committees concerned with education and the progress of women. He traveled widely in service to the Faith to Europe, Turkey, the Middle East, India, Pakistan, and Afghanistan. He was an eloquent speaker and a renowned scholar, the editor-in-chief of the national Iranian Bahá'í journal, and one of the founders and a regular contributor to the Bahá'í Women's Journal and the Youth Magazine.[21]

Excited by the apparent congruence of ideas between the Bahá'í view of peace and the contents of the newspaper article, and aware that the Central Organization was interested in promoting widespread discussion and study of the conditions underlying a sustainable peace, Aḥmad Yazdání decided to seize the opportunity to bring to the attention of the Organization a number of additional elements for its consideration—in particular, "the need for the treatment of the spiritual and fundamental causes of war, as well as the solutions needed for a true long-lasting spiritually-based peace."[22]

In implementing his plan, Yazdání sought the assistance of two senior and well-connected Bahá'ís. The first was the eminent scholar Jináb-i-Ibn-i-Aṣdaq, Mírzá Alí-Muḥammad (1850–1928), who was given the high rank of Hand of the Cause of God for his outstanding services to the Bahá'í Faith.[23] The second was Colonel Ibráhím Pírúzbakht (1978–1937).[24] Both of these men were familiar with world events, had traveled widely, and had contact with prominent people in the upper echelons of society.

Ibn-i-Aṣdaq traveled widely in service to the Faith and visited many parts of Persia, Iraq, India, Burma, and Caucasia, as well as Ashkhabad and Marv in Turkmenistan. He was a member of the first Central Spiritual Assembly established at 'Abdu'l-Bahá's direction in Tehran in 1897. During his lifetime, he frequently visited Bahá'u'lláh and 'Abdu'l-Bahá in Palestine. The latter entrusted him with various tasks such as the presentation of His *Risáliy-i-Siyásíyyih* ("Treatise on Politics" written in 1893) to the Shah of Persia, to contemporary religious authorities, and to Persian notables. His wife, a great-granddaughter of Muḥammad S͟háh, was the sister-in-law of Enteẓám-al-Salṭana, a socially prominent Bahá'í. Such was his distinguished service to the Bahá'í Faith that Shoghi Effendi, the Guardian of the Faith, reckoned Ibn-i-Aṣdaq the nineteenth of the nineteen Apostles of Bahá'u'lláh.[25]

The second person drawn into the consultation was Colonel Ibráhím Pírúzbakht, who was educated as a physician and served in senior positions in the Iranian military. Born in Tehran, he studied in Russia, France, and Belgium, and he received his diploma in medicine, surgery, and midwifery from the Liège School in Belgium in 1907. He began to investigate the Bahá'í religion in 1914 and was subsequently appointed to the Spiritual Assembly of Tehran in 1919 and to the position of Chief of the prestigious Bahá'í Tarbiyát School for Boys. His high position in the military brought him in contact with people of influence, whom he was able to acquaint with the importance of the Bahá'í Faith and the great material and moral benefits that the principles of the Faith rendered to the country of Iran and to the world.[26]

Aḥmad Yazdání describes the way in which they proceeded in initiating contact with the Executive Committee. Following consultation, they "prepared and translated [into French] some articles, sent them to the executive committee of the Organization, and shared with them the principles of the establishment of true peace, in order to encourage them to seek inspiration and assistance in this regard from 'Abdu'l-Bahá. After an exchange of several communications with the committee, several letters addressed to 'Abdu'l-Bahá were received in Ṭihrán to be delivered to Him. Nevertheless, the delivery of these letters was delayed until after the war ended . . ."[27]

As previously noted, since 'Abdu'l-Bahá resided in the Holy Land, and since Palestine, then an outpost of the Ottoman Empire, had entered the war on the side of Germany, the delivery of these letters had to be delayed until after the end of World War I. For the duration of the war, the population of Palestine was subject to severe privations and hardships. The area was isolated, and communication with the rest of the world, by mail and other means, was periodically cut off.

Aḥmad Yazdání states that once the war had ended and communication with the Holy Land had been restored, Ibn-i-Aṣdaq cabled 'Abdu'l-Bahá seeking permission to travel to the Holy Land. When approval was received, Ibn-i-Aṣdaq immediately departed for Haifa, arriving early in December, 1919. He took with him, for presentation to 'Abdu'l-Bahá, the letter the Iranian Bahá'ís had addressed to the Executive Committee of the Organization for a Durable Peace and the Committee's letters addressed to 'Abdu'l-Bahá, which had been sent during the war to Iran in care of the Iranian Bahá'ís for forwarding to 'Abdu'l-Bahá.

On receipt of this material from Ibn-i-Aṣdaq, 'Abdu'l-Bahá wrote a detailed Tablet to the Executive Committee on December 17, 1919.[28] He addressed its members as "O ye esteemed ones who are pioneers among the well-wishers of the world of humanity," and an opening paragraph explained, "The letters which ye sent during the war were not received, but a letter dated February 11th, 1916, has just come to hand, and immediately an answer is being written."[29]

To ensure the safe delivery of His Tablet, 'Abdu'l-Bahá subsequently appointed a delegation and entrusted its members, Ibn-i-Aṣdaq and Aḥmad Yazdání, with the mission of traveling to The Hague to deliver His letter into the hands of the Committee.[30]

The Delegation

Ibn-i-Aṣdaq reached the Holy Land around December 1919; however, Aḥmad Yazdání did not arrive until April 1920. Yazdání states that it was not until a few days after his arrival that he became aware he "had been summoned in order to deliver the detailed Tablet and its English translation, which had been prepared by Shoghi Effendi, Dr. Esslemont, Díyá Baghdádí and Luṭfu'lláh Ḥakím, and that . . . [he] was to accompany Jináb-i-Ibn-i-Aṣdaq and hand deliver it."[31]

After studying the contents of the Tablet, Ibn-i-Aṣdaq and Aḥmad Yazdání gained a deeper appreciation of the importance of this document, which in simple yet eloquent and profound language set out the Baháʼí principles on peace and clearly explained how the countries of the world should go about electing representatives to the Supreme Tribunal, which had been called for in the Writings of Baháʼu'lláh. Ibn-i-Aṣdaq and Aḥmad Yazdání also understood the significance of their assignment. They had been commissioned to carry the historic letter of ʻAbduʼl-Bahá to the Netherlands, to ensure personally that it was placed in the hands of the Executive Committee of the Central Organization for a Durable Peace in The Hague, and to submit a report of what transpired to ʻAbduʼl-Bahá.

During their stay in Haifa, ʻAbduʼl-Bahá prepared Ibn-i-Aṣdaq and Aḥmad Yazdání for their assignment, and He offered encouragement and guidance of a spiritual nature. In May 1920, the two emissaries departed, armed with ʻAbduʼl-Bahá's letter and its English translation. They traveled to Egypt, where they boarded a boat to Rotterdam, the Netherlands. The journey from Haifa to The Hague took eleven days.

The arrival of two Oriental men in the Netherlands created quite a stir. Ibn-i-Aṣdaq and Aḥmad Yazdání made a very unusual-looking pair. One was a bearded elderly man in long Eastern attire; the other was very young, clean-shaven, and wearing a business suit and a European-style hat. As they walked around the city, people stared, pointed, and wondered where they had come from and why they were there. Some assumed they were Turks. In one of the towns they visited, their presence created quite a disturbance. A large friendly crowd gathered round them, laughing, jostling, wanting to get close to them, and the police had to be called to disperse the group of curious citizens.[32]

Upon their arrival in The Hague, they set out to find the office of the Executive Committee of the Central Organization for a Durable Peace. Aḥmad Yazdání reports that it was no easy task since they did not speak Dutch, and the peace group had changed its meeting place many times. They ultimately discovered that the Organization had disbanded at the end of the war and that a new one had taken its place. All that remained of the Executive Committee was its local president, vice president, and secretary. Yazdání alludes to the challenge of locating the office of the Executive Committee, and he describes the surprised reaction of its secretary to the unexpected appearance of two men from Iran: "After searching for a few days, we were able to find the office of the Executive Committee. There, we only found the secretary. We explained to her about the purpose of our journey and the Tablet with which we were entrusted. Clearly, they were surprised to receive such guests. They could not imagine that following the several-years-old correspondence between us, there was anyone who would care so much about the subject of peace as to dispatch two individuals from a land as far away as Iran to exchange ideas about the topic—and that we were doing this two years after the war had ended."[33]

The secretary, Mrs. A. J. Dyserinck,[34] referred Ibn-i-Aṣdaq and Aḥmad Yazdání to the President of the Executive Committee, Dr. H. C. Dresselhuys (1870–1926),[35] who was then serving as a member of the Parliament in the Netherlands. Yazdání went to the Parliament building to meet him and to explain their mission. "Since he was very busy," Yazdání explains, "he politely referred me back to the same Executive Committee Office, assuring me that he would give instructions for the receipt and perusal of the Tablet."[36]

Reflecting on the reaction of the Committee members to the unexpected arrival of the delegation, Aḥmad Yazdání observes: "I then realized that the Committee had not been meeting as often as it used to, and that their universal peace initiative had been dissolved owing to the end of the war and the temporary peace now in place, which had given them no reason to follow up. It became even clearer to us when Jináb-i-Ibn-i-Aṣdaq and I met with the

Deputy President of the Committee at a specific location and delivered the Tablet and its translation to him, that their interest in universal peace was fundamentally in pursuit of image and driven by political motives."[37]

Delivery of the First Hague Tablet

The delegation delivered 'Abdu'l-Bahá's letter of December 17, 1919 to the Deputy President of the Executive Committee of the Central Organization for a Durable Peace early in June 1920. Attached to His December 17 letter, 'Abdu'l-Bahá provided, for the information of the Executive Committee, a copy of another relevant Tablet, addressed to the people of the world, regarding the teachings of Bahá'u'lláh, which He had written "some time ago, during the war."[38]

The contents of the December 17 letter to the Executive Committee of the Central Organization will be examined in a later chapter. Briefly, while acknowledging the pioneering contribution of the Organization, 'Abdu'l-Bahá's Tablet places the attainment of international peace within the context of the need for wider political, economic, and cultural change. He explains basic principles of the Faith, cautions the Executive Committee that other people might come from the East presenting these teachings as their own, elaborates on the subject of universal peace, offers to collaborate with the Committee, and points out a number of factors limiting the effective operation of the newly established League of Nations. His letter drew the organizers' attention to Bahá'u'lláh's enunciation of spiritual truths that provide a foundation for the realization of their Organization's aims: "O ye esteemed ones who are pioneers among the well-wishers of the world of humanity! . . . At present universal peace is a matter of great importance, but unity of conscience is essential, so that the foundation of this matter may become secure, its establishment firm and its edifice strong. . . ."[39]

On June 12, 1920, a few days after receiving 'Abdu'l-Bahá's Tablet, Dr. Dresselhuys, the President of the Executive Committee, responded in French to the letter from 'Abdu'l-Bahá. Aḥmad Yazdání immediately translated the Committee's letter into Persian and forwarded it to 'Abdu'l-Bahá in the Holy Land.[40]

The Executive Committee's letter of reply to 'Abdu'l-Bahá was signed by Dr. Dresselhuys and was cordial in tone. The letter expressed the appreciation of the Committee that the leader of an international movement, with followers in all parts of the world, had such a high regard for the importance of the work of the Executive Committee that He arranged for two of its representatives to undertake the long journey from Iran to the Netherlands to deliver His message. The letter states that the message conveyed by the delegation—namely, that the cause of peace is a cause of such importance that it is necessary to work for it always—is endorsed by the Committee, and is one for which they continue to work. It identifies the members of the Committee as representatives of the pacifist movement and expresses pleasure that the pacifist doctrine forms part of the principles of a religion that has such a great number of followers who show such admirable faith and fervor. Referring to 'Abdu'l-Bahá's desire to collaborate with the Organization, while leaving the door open to possible collaboration and offering to share their information and experience concerning the European pacifist movement and the development of the League of Nations, the letter identifies several issues which might preclude cooperation. For example, the Committee notes that while universal peace is important to both the Executive Committee and the Bahá'ís, the pacificism to which the members of the Executive Committee subscribe does not embrace the twelve principles that form part of the Bahá'í program, and opinions are divided among pacifists concerning religious and political issues.

Disappointed with the reaction of the Executive Committee to 'Abdu'l-Bahá's lengthy Tablet, Aḥmad Yazdání came to the conclusion that "they had misunderstood the driving motive behind our correspondence with them, the Tablet of 'Abdu'l-Bahá, and our journey, to be an attempt to use the Organization for the promotion of our Cause."[41]

As instructed by 'Abdu'l-Bahá, Ibn-i-Aṣdaq and Aḥmad Yazdání each shared their observations with 'Abdu'l-Bahá in letters dated June 14, 1920.

From these reports, it appeared that they had concluded that the effort to engage in communication with the Central Organization had proven futile since the minds of its members were now focused elsewhere and they were occupied with other matters.

However, 'Abdu'l-Bahá advised them to retain cordial and good relations with the Organization and to redirect their energies toward other areas of service. His perspective on the matter can be gleaned from His response to Aḥmad Yazdání's letter of June 14, 1920, an excerpt from which is cited below.[42] 'Abdu'l-Bahá's view is more nuanced and placed within the context of the importance of understanding the challenges associated with engaging in discourses on pressing social issues. In His Tablet, 'Abdu'l-Bahá begins by informing Aḥmad Yazdání that he had received the June 12, 1920 letter from members of the Executive Committee and had written a second Tablet in answer to the Committee's letter. 'Abdu'l-Bahá instructs Yazdání to deliver the second Tablet to them.

'Abdu'l-Bahá's Tablet to Yazdání reflects more broadly on the challenges confronting groups that are endeavoring to promote peace; He foreshadows another and more terrible war in the future; and he provides specific guidance concerning a future meeting with the members of the Executive Committee. 'Abdu'l-Bahá writes:

> It is evident that this meeting is not what it is reputed to be and is unable to order and arrange affairs in the manner which is befitting and necessary. However that may be, the matter in which they are engaged is nevertheless of the greatest importance. The meeting at The Hague should have such power and influence that its word will have an effect on the governments and nations. Point out to the revered members gathered there that the Hague Conference[43] held before the war had as its President the Emperor of Russia, and its members were men of the greatest eminence. Nevertheless this did not prevent such a terrible war. Now how will it be? For in the future another war, fiercer than the last,

will assuredly break out; verily, of this there is no doubt whatever. What can the Hague meeting do?

But the fundamental principles laid down by Bahá'u'lláh are day by day spreading. Deliver the answer to their letter and express the greatest love and kindness, and leave them to their own affairs. In any case they ought to be pleased with you, and subject to their approval you may print and distribute that detailed epistle of mine which hath already been translated into English.[44]

At the end of His Tablet, 'Abdu'l-Bahá suggests that, as a keen Esperantist, Yazdání redirect his energies towards a more receptive group and associate with the Dutch Esperanto groups during his visit to The Netherlands. He also encourages Aḥmad Yazdání to maintain good ties with the Central Organization of a Durable Peace at The Hague.

Delivery of the Second Hague Tablet

In reply to the letter dated June 12, 1920 from the Executive Committee, 'Abdu'l-Bahá on July 1, 1920 addressed a second and shorter Tablet to The Hague Committee. The second Tablet to The Hague is included as item 2 in Appendix 2. 'Abdu'l-Bahá's letter emphasized the high regard in which Bahá'ís held "esteemed members of the Executive Committee of the Central Organization for a Durable Peace." He stressed the common vision shared by the Bahá'ís and the Central Organization and underlined the link between the prosperity of humankind and the attainment of Universal Peace. The letter states:

Your reply, dated 12 June 1920, to my letter was received with the utmost gratitude. God be praised, it testified to the unity of thought and purpose that existeth between us and you, and expressed sentiments of the heart that bear the hallmark of sincere affection.

We Bahá'ís have the greatest affinity for your esteemed organization, and dispatched therefore two distinguished individuals to you in order to forge a strong bond. For in this day the cause of universal peace is of paramount importance amongst all human affairs and is the greatest instrument for securing the very life and felicity of mankind. Bereft of this effulgent reality, humanity can in no wise find true composure or real advancement but will, day by day, sink ever deeper into misery and wretchedness.[45]

This second Tablet from 'Abdu'l-Bahá was delivered to the Executive Committee by Ibn-i-Aṣdaq and Aḥmad Yazdání. Following this meeting, Yazdání reported, "they did not respond, and we did not meet with them again . . ."[46] No additional information is available about what transpired.

A Third Tablet

A manuscript copy of a third Tablet addressed by 'Abdu'l-Bahá to the Central Organization through Mrs. A. J. Dyserinck, the secretary, is published in its original language—Persian—on page 18 of volume 4 of *Makátíb-i-Ḥaḍrat-i-'Abdu'l-Bahá*. The manuscript bears no date, and an authorized English translation of the Tablet is, to date, not available. No additional historical information about the Tablet has so far been located. It is also not known whether the third Tablet might have been mailed or delivered to the Organization in The Hague.

In the absence of an authorized English translation of this Tablet, we provide the following brief summary of some of its major themes: 'Abdu'l-Bahá begins by praising the contribution of the Executive Committee's noble thoughts and lofty intentions in the pursuit of universal peace; He affirms that the peace and tranquility of the world depend upon improving the character of man and that the greatest means for training man to possess praiseworthy characteristics are noble aspirations and the expansion of the mind. He observes that humankind is narrowly focused on its own self-interest, and He comments on the impact this perspective has on social inequality and the relationship between nations, and its potential to promote conflict.

He calls for the compass of the individual's thinking to be expanded beyond self-gain—in order to recognize that the basis of the prosperity of every member of his species lies in the gain of all mankind—and to appreciate that the injury of any nation or state is the same as an injury to his own nation and state. 'Abdu'l-Bahá contrasts this view to the present state of the world, where nations are focused on how to advance their own interests while working against the best interests of other nations. He calls for cooperation—rather than a struggle—among nations for survival, and He encourages a change in human consciousness, imbued with moral and spiritual values, capable of improving human character and giving expression to equality, fellowship, and a willingness to sacrifice one's self for the sake of one's fellow-man. He expresses the hope that the members of the Executive Committee, because of their dedication to the welfare of humanity, will become the cause of training humankind to acquire the universal virtues necessary to change human consciousness and transform the world.

Concluding Comments

How to assess the significance of the events described above? From a mere statement of the facts, it would be easy to conclude that the result of the communication was negligible. While the Central Organization and its Executive Committee had been actively involved in promoting serious study and planning concerning the fundamental requirements for a sustainable and universal peace, its efforts had been overtaken by the establishment of the League of Nations, and, unbeknownst to the Bahá'í delegation from Iran, the Central Organization had already largely disbanded before the meetings with the Bahá'í delegation took place.

From a historical perspective, it is interesting that a religion, in this case, the Bahá'í Faith—which is devoted to the promotion of universal peace, justice, and equality; which has its origins in nineteenth century Iran; and which from its earliest days suffered violent persecution in the land of its birth for its modern perspective and global embrace—accorded such importance to the work of the Central Organization for a Durable Peace at The Hague. This was an informal international group formed in 1915 that had little more than nonbinding moral force and that was subsequently superseded by the formation of the League of Nations. What is unique about this situation is that the head of the religion, residing in the Holy Land, sent a delegation of two men from Iran to the Netherlands to deliver a detailed letter to the Executive Committee for the purpose of furthering widespread discussion about the vital subject of universal peace and the means for its attainment.

It is also noteworthy that the initial contact between the Iranian Bahá'ís and the Executive Committee began in 1915, when the world—including Iran—was in the throes of the First World War. Though intermittent, this contact continued until 1920. The interaction was the result of personal initiative. The communication, which was done by mail and conducted in French, was set in motion by informed individuals who were concerned about the state of the world, clearly saw the need for peace, and were conscious of the fundamental changes in attitude required to achieve a lasting peace. They were willing to make the effort to share their understandings as a contribution to promoting a discussion of peace and as a means of sharing information about new sources of ideas. It was to this end that they suggested that the Executive Committee communicate with 'Abdu'l-Bahá.

Finally, though Aḥmad Yazdání had clearly hoped for a more immediate positive outcome, with the encouragement of 'Abdu'l-Bahá, and prior to leaving the Netherlands, he obtained the agreement of the Executive Committee to publish and distribute the English translation of the First and Second Tablet to The Hague. In addition, with the assistance of a Professor of Linguistics, a booklet about the Bahá'í teachings was published in Dutch. Yazdání, when it became known that he was an Esperantist, was invited to become involved with The Hague Esperanto Group, thus affording him many opportunities to promote the important subject of peace.[47]

But, might the above events have a longer-term significance? What can be learned for contemporary times? In the final chapters we consider present-day orientations to peace in the light of the contents of the historic Tablets 'Abdu'l-Bahá addressed to the Central Organization for a Durable Peace at The Hague, and we examine the challenges of achieving global peace.

7 / Analysis of the Tablets to The Hague

When the hostilities ceased in November 1918, and the battlefields fell silent, statesmen and politicians hastened to Paris to participate in the Peace Conference.[1] With the intense suffering and unprecedented bloodshed still vivid in their memories, they gathered with the intention of laying the foundations of a new order capable of bringing stability and lasting peace to the world.

'Abdu'l-Bahá's Tablets to the Executive Committee of the Central Organization for a Durable Peace at The Hague were penned in 1919–1920 at the time the Peace Conference in Paris was in the process of finalizing agreement on the details of the peace treaty and the nature of the international agency destined to administer its provisions. These letters, which were written from Palestine, exemplify 'Abdu'l-Bahá's commitment to engaging with groups in the wider society who were actively involved in promoting international peace and to fostering public discourse on the subject of peace.

In this chapter, we briefly outline the unfoldment of attempts to achieve peace at the end of World War I, as a context within which to explore the enduring contribution of the contents of 'Abdu'l-Bahá's Tablets to the Executive Committee to the attainment of peace in contemporary times. And, in the final chapter, we examine what remains to be done to attain peace.

Initial Steps Toward Peace

Reflecting on the origins of the new conceptions of international relations that emerged from Versailles in 1919, historian, Ronald Stromberg observes that "Of the great ideas which have captured men's imagination, in the modern democratic age at least, most have arisen from some urgent emotional need, not from a strictly rational analysis."[2] Taking as an example, the concept of collective security, Stromberg captures the tension between the popular appeal of the idea and the lack of political will to adopt it. Concerning the concept of collective security, he asserts that, "certainly," it ". . . did not come from the more experienced diplomats and statesmen, who were in the main quite skeptical about it. It came from journalists, moralists, popular politicians, from 'the people'; it responded to a cry of protest against the intolerable existence of world war and a demand for reassurance that such wars be not permitted to happen again. This popular and unsophisticated call for the abolition of war insistently required some visible sign of a wholly new spirit. The planners of peace had to contrive some scheme to meet this demand, and they scurried about rather frantically trying to make reason match emotion."[3]

The unprecedented loss of life occasioned by World War I and the accompanying widespread social and economic dislocation that occurred gave rise to a growing public demand that some method be found to prevent the renewal of the suffering and destruction that were now seen to be an inescapable part of modern warfare. The spirit of the times was personified in the President of the United States, Woodrow Wilson, who pushed toward the creation of a more comprehensive global organization that would include all independent states and in which even the smallest state would have a voice.[4] The force of this demand was so strong that within a few weeks after the opening of the Paris Peace Conference in January, 1919, unanimous agreement had been reached on the text of the Covenant of the League of Nations, a new organization created to promote international cooperation and to achieve peace and security. Established at the initiative of the victorious Allied powers at the end of World War I, the League of Nations was an integral feature of the Treaty of Versailles. The signing of the Treaty in Paris in January 1920 marked the formal end of the First World War.

Treaty of Versailles: Ambivalent Motivations—Settlement vs Peace

When the delegates convened at the Paris Peace Conference, it did not take long before conflicting motives began to emerge and color their discussions. While it was generally agreed that the new international order should be capable of ensuring future peace, the victorious Allies were also intent on exacting reparations from the vanquished nations. Deliberations, from which the Germans were largely excluded, proceeded on two fronts, both of which are embodied in the provisions of the final Treaty of Versailles. "Despite months of wrangling over colonies, borders, and clauses in the text of the peace treaty, the Versailles settlement eventually incorporated an attenuated form of the proposed League of Nations, an institution which it was hoped could adjust future disputes between nations and harmonize international affairs."[5]

The eventual treaty included fifteen parts and 440 articles. Part I created the Covenant of the new League of Nations, which Germany was not permitted to join until 1926. The remaining sections of the treaty focused, to a large extent, specifically on delimiting the power of the defeated nations and assigning liability for reparations. For example, the Treaty of Versailles specified Germany's new boundaries, stipulated a demilitarized zone, and separated the Saar from Germany for fifteen years. It stripped Germany of all its colonies, reduced her armed forces to very low levels, prohibited Germany from possessing certain classes of weapons, and also committing the Allies to eventual disarmament as well. In addition, the treaty imposed numerous financial obligations upon the defeated: Though technically the treaty did not declare Germany alone as guilty for causing the war—a war for which all parties had been, to one degree or another responsible—it established Germany's liability for reparations to be paid to the Allies for the losses and damages suffered as a result of the aggression of Germany and her allies.

After strict enforcement of the treaty for five years, the French assented to the modification of important provisions. Germany agreed to pay reparations under the Dawes Plan and the Young Plan, but those plans were canceled in 1932, and Hitler's rise to power and subsequent actions rendered moot the remaining terms of the treaty.[6]

The League of Nations

The first section (Part 1) of the Treaty of Versailles created the Covenant of the new League of Nations.[7] Writing about the idea of this new institution historian Charles Townshend observed that the League of Nations aimed

> . . . to eliminate four fatal flaws of the old European states: in place of competing monarchical empires—of which the Hapsburg Empire was perhaps the most notorious—the principle of national self-determination would create a world of independent nation states, free of outside interference; the secret diplomacy of the old order would be replaced by the open discussion and resolution of disputes; the military alliance blocs would be replaced by a system of collective guarantees of security; and agreed disarmament would prevent the recurrence of the kind of arms race that had racked up international tensions in the pre-war decade.[8]

The forces that contributed to the establishment of and gave direction to the shape of the Covenant and the structure of the League of Nations included collective security, arbitration, economic and social cooperation, reduction of armaments, and open diplomacy: "These general propositions . . . inspired in various degrees the plans drawn up during the war. It was urged from the first that they could become effective only through the creation of a great international organization charged with the duty of applying them and invested with the powers necessary to that end."[9]

Central to the deliberations of the delegates was the principle of collective security—a system, regional or global, in which each state in the system accepts that the security of one is the concern of all and agrees to join in a collective response to threats to and breaches of the peace. Collective security is a means of crisis management; war or aggression is viewed as a breach of international peace and security, and collective security stands for collective action by all the nations in defense of peace. As noted above, the premise of collective security was, for practical purposes, a new concept engendered by the unprecedented pressures of World War I.[10]

Several features of the League of Nations were developed from existing institutions or from time-honored proposals for the reform of previous diplomatic methods. For example, The Hague Conferences of 1899 and 1907 had given careful consideration to plans for the settlement of disputes between states by legal means or, failing these, by third-party arbitration. The results had, however, been unimpressive, due in part to the prevailing traditional view that there was no natural or supreme law by which the rights of sovereign states, including that of making war as and when they chose, could be judged or limited. The 1907 Hague Conference tried unsuccessfully to set up an international court, and though many arbitration treaties were signed between individual states, they all contained reservations that precluded their more general application. Nevertheless, the general principle of arbitration had become widely accepted by public opinion and was embodied as a matter of course in the Covenant.[11]

While the Covenant professed to cover such issues of collective security; arbitration and judicial settlement, including the creation of an international court; international cooperation or control in economic and social affairs; disarmament; and open diplomacy, it did not satisfy extreme pacifists—who rejected any use of force (even to resist aggression)—or extreme internation-alists, who wished the League to have its own military forces and to impose all its decisions by its own political and military authority.[12]

At the opening of the Peace Conference in Paris in 1919, expectations had been high. It was generally agreed that the conference's task should include the establishment of a League of Nations capable of ensuring the future peace of the world. Historian Firuz Kazemzadeh observed:

> . . . the formation of a League of Nations was enthusiastically welcomed by the masses and reluctantly followed by the leaders. However, the League of Nations was a purely political institution, a loose and far from universal association of sovereign states each of which reserved to itself the ultimate power to wage war. A vast majority of those who met at the Paris Peace Conference in 1919 paid lip service to the cause of peace while placing the narrow and selfish interests of their respec-tive nations, classes, and parties above the interests of humanity. At the conference table, and in the crowded corridors, "the peacemakers" sowed the seeds of future conflicts. To them peacemaking had no spiri-tual dimension and they did not address themselves to the deeper levels in the nature of man.[13]

While the actions taken by the League fell short of the hopes of its founders, its creation was an event of decisive importance in the history of international relations, as it set in motion a breadth of measures—legal, social, economic, and institutional—that were intended to safeguard and broker peace but that experience later showed were inherently flawed. For example, although the League included such features as a legislature, a judiciary, an executive, and a supporting bureaucracy, it had been denied the authority vital to the work it was ostensibly intended to perform. Locked into the nineteenth century's conception of untrammeled national sovereignty, it could take decisions only with the unanimous assent of the member states.

The League was further weakened by "its failure to include in its membership some of the world's most powerful states: Germany had been rejected as a defeated nation held responsible for the war, Russia was initially denied entrance because of its Bolshevik regime, and the United States itself refused—as a result of narrow political partisanship in Congress—either to join the League or to ratify the treaty."[14] In addition, the League had no power either to enforce its covenant (apart from the ability of member states to take united and determined action against a belligerent state) or to intervene in acts of aggression by one state against another. As a consequence, its failure to prevent Japanese expansion in Manchuria and China (1931 to 1933), Italy's conquest of Ethiopia (1935), or Hitler's repudiation of the Versailles Treaty in 1933 thoroughly discredited the League and rendered it powerless to avert World War II. The League of Nations was formally disbanded on April 19, 1946; and its powers and functions were transferred to the nascent United Nations Organization.

Tablets to The Hague: Implications for Discourse

An astute observer of world affairs, 'Abdu'l-Bahá was well-informed of the events of the day—the goals of the Peace Conference, the power plays of competing empires, and their potential impacts on the conditions of life of the people. It is clear from His Writings that 'Abdu'l-Bahá was aware of the formation of the League of Nations and that He was familiar with the details of its administrative structure.[15] The Tablets to the Executive Committee of the Central Organization for a Durable Peace at The Hague were written at the time the Peace Conference in Paris was finalizing the details of the peace treaty and the nature of the international agency destined to administer its provisions.

While the content of His Tablets to The Hague resonate with contemporary issues, they do not represent a detailed commentary on the events of the day; rather, they raise and embed the discussion of peace in a new and elevated context. They demonstrate 'Abdu'l-Bahá's commitment to engaging with groups in the wider society—who were actively involved in promoting international peace—and to fostering public discourse on the subject of peace. The solutions He offers are directed toward laying the foundations for a sustainable peace by eliminating the causes of war. The content of the Tablets is challenging and wide ranging. Their overall approach is to provide information about the broad Bahá'í conception of peace, to broaden understanding, and to identify common ground. The Tablets open the way for further discussion. While avoiding fruitless conflict, naïve, and simplistic prescriptions, they strive to unite people in the search for underlying moral and spiritual principles and for practical measures conducive to the just resolution of the problems afflicting society.

The Tablets to the Executive Committee at The Hague were composed in response to specific questions and comments from a group of highly respected individuals who were involved in the promotion of international peace and who had been actively endeavoring to generate widespread public discussion and study of the prerequisites for a sustainable peace.

Taking into consideration Bahá'u'lláh's pronouncement that a "different Cause" has appeared in this day and that "a different discourse is required,"[16] 'Abdu'l-Bahá chooses to embed the subject of peace within a broader historical context and to underline its spiritual foundation. He links the discussion of peace to events that took place in the Orient in the middle of the nineteenth century. His focus is on the advent of Bahá'u'lláh. He describes His teachings, His imprisonment and exiles, and sets out the central focus of Bahá'u'lláh's mission—namely, the realization of the oneness of humankind and the establishment of peace among the nations. 'Abdu'l-Bahá offers the experience of the Bahá'í community in Iran at that time as an example of the transformative power of these spiritual and moral teachings when put into practice in daily life. Writing in the first Tablet, He states:

> Therefore Bahá'u'lláh, fifty years ago, expounded this question of universal peace at a time when He was confined in the fortress of 'Akká

132

and was wronged and imprisoned. He wrote about this important matter of universal peace to all the great sovereigns of the world, and established it among His friends in the Orient. The horizon of the East was in utter darkness, nations displayed the utmost hatred and enmity towards each other, religions thirsted for each other's blood, and it was darkness upon darkness. At such a time Bahá'u'lláh shone forth like the sun from the horizon of the east and illumined Persia with the lights of these teachings.[17]

And, in the second Tablet to The Hague, while emphasizing the underlying moral and spiritual nature of peace, He comments, "our desire for peace is not derived merely from the intellect: It is a matter of religious belief and one of the eternal foundations of the Faith of God."[18]

'Abdu'l-Bahá's Tablets stress the complexity of the Bahá'í conception of peace, which is best understood within the context of the entirety of the Bahá'í teachings, and He informs the Central Organization that the teachings of Bahá'u'lláh, announced over fifty years ago,[19] supplement and support the idea of peace. These teachings constitute an enlarged framework for peace and illustrate the breadth and complexity of the initiatives that are necessary to create an environment conducive to the development of a sustainable universal peace and to the emergence of international institutions capable of preserving global peace.

In the following sections, we highlight some of the themes contained in the first and second Tablets to the Executive Committee.

The First Tablet, Dated December 17, 1919

'Abdu'l-Bahá in the first Tablet, acknowledges the work of the members of the Executive Committee. He contrasts the evils of war with the benefits of universal peace and describes the impact of the recent war on the frame of mind of the general population and the thinkers of the world. "There is not one soul," He states, "whose conscience does not testify that in this day there is no more important matter in the world than that of universal peace."[20] Commenting on this widespread view, He observes that the leaders of humanity have generally conceived of peace in purely political terms, and He notes that this narrowly focused approach has proven insufficient to achieving a lasting peace. The essential missing ingredient, He asserts, is "unity of conscience"—the need for peace to be built on a broader consensus and for its pursuit to include the resolution of issues that currently constitute barriers to peace and that are not commonly associated with the quest for peace. He writes, "But the wise souls who are aware of the essential relationships emanating from the realities of things consider that one single matter cannot, by itself, influence the human reality as it ought and should, for until the minds of men become united, no important matter can be accomplished. At present universal peace is a matter of great importance, but unity of conscience is essential, so that the foundation of this matter may become secure, its establishment firm and its edifice strong."[21]

The concept of "unity of conscience" in the passage above appears to involve two interrelated dimensions, each of which underpins moral social responsibility and requires action. On the one hand, "unity of conscience" relates to the acquisition of knowledge in order to gain an understanding of the complex, multifaceted organic nature of the present world in which humankind resides. To this end, Bahá'u'lláh compares the world to a human body that, although whole, suffers from multiple disorders and maladies.[22] Therefore, "unity of conscience" implies awareness of the "essential relationships" that bind together the elements of human society and of the barriers that stand in the way of peace. In order to achieve unity in "the minds of men" on the "important matter" of the pursuit of peace, what is required is unity of thought and action around a set of principles.

The term "unity of conscience" also suggests the development of ethics and moral purpose that relate to motivation and the will to engage in action that creates an environment conducive to peace. The process gives rise to a sense of duty and acceptance of a moral responsibility to work to promote not only universal peace but also to labor more broadly for the common good.[23]

To illustrate the importance of the notion of "unity of conscience," 'Abdu'l-Bahá refers to the essential relationship between the establishment of universal peace and the acceptance and practice of certain supplemental society-building teachings promulgated by Bahá'u'lláh in the latter part of the nineteenth century. He acquaints The Hague Committee with the significant changes in consciousness occurring in "the minds of men" that resulted from embracing this broader approach to peace: "Among His [Bahá'u'lláh's] teachings was the declaration of universal peace. People of different nations, religions and sects who followed Him came together to such an extent that remarkable gatherings were instituted consisting of the various nations and religions of the East. Every soul who entered these gatherings saw but one nation, one teaching, one pathway, one order, for the teachings of Bahá'u'lláh were not limited to the establishment of universal peace. They embraced many teachings which supplemented and supported that of universal peace."[24]

In the pursuit of peace, the underlying aim of the Bahá'ís is to reconcile, to heal divisions, to bring about mutual respect among men. Elsewhere, 'Abdu'l-Bahá states, ". . . peace must first be established among individuals, until it leadeth in the end to peace among nations."[25] Addressing the Bahá'ís, He calls upon them to take responsibility for the peace and wellbeing of society. "Strive ye," He writes, "with all your might to create, through the power of the Word of God, genuine love, spiritual communion and durable bonds among individuals. This is your task."[26] The teachings of Bahá'u'lláh provide an enlarged context for achieving a universal consciousness. They remove barriers that hinder the realization of peace and lay the foundations for a peaceful and universal society. The process of transformation set in motion "advances by inducing a fundamental change of consciousness, and the challenge it poses to everyone who would serve it is to free oneself from attachment to inherited assumptions and preferences that are irreconcilable with the Will of God for humanity's coming of age."[27]

'Abdu'l-Bahá's statements concerning the pursuit of peace—in particular the need for a broad consensus, rather than agreement on a single issue—suggest that peace requires a unity of thought that sees peace as being dependent on the transformation of many aspects of culture and social institutions.

Returning to the text of the first Tablet to The Hague—having established the importance of "unity of conscience," 'Abdu'l-Bahá provides a detailed discussion of various foundational teachings of Bahá'u'lláh that pertain to the principle of the oneness of humankind and define preconditions for peace. Aware that the formulation of specific action strategies is necessarily dependent on the exigencies of time and place, 'Abdu'l-Bahá addresses the issue of peace at the level of moral principle rather than outline precise action strategies. Included among these principles He enumerates are the independent investigation of "reality so that the world of humanity may be saved from the darkness of imitation and attain to the truth;"[28] the recognition of the oneness of the world of humanity; and the belief that religion must be the cause of fellowship and love. Indeed, He states, "If it [religion] becomes the cause of estrangement then it is not needed, for religion is like a remedy; if it aggravates the disease then it becomes unnecessary."[29] He asserts that religion must be in conformity with science and reason "so that it may influence the hearts of men."[30] He also asserts that religious, racial, political, national, economic, and patriotic prejudices destroy the edifice of human society. Prejudices must, therefore, be abandoned for peace to be attained.

The Tablet itemizes a number of central teachings conducive to unity and social development that are among the prerequisites and critical to the attainment of peace. 'Abdu'l-Bahá includes, for example, the need for a universal auxiliary language as a means of eliminating misunderstandings in communicating on vital matters among mankind; the equality of women and men; the voluntary sharing of one's property with others; the freedom to develop the distinctly human part of man's nature and spirit; and the role of religion in ensuring social order, provided that "by religion is meant that which is ascertained by investigation and not that which is based on mere imitation."[31] 'Abdu'l-Bahá identifies, as pressing requirements of the day, the need for present-day material civilization to be combined with spiritual and moral values ("Divine civilization") in order to enhance its benefits to humanity and the promotion of education. And He underlines the importance of "justice and right," without which "all things shall be in disorder and remain imperfect."[32]

'Abdu'l-Bahá explains the critical relationship to social well-being and the realization of peace of the numerous and "manifold principles" of Bahá'u'lláh. He mentions in His Tablet:

> These manifold principles, which constitute the greatest basis for the felicity of mankind and are of the bounties of the Merciful, must be added to the matter of universal peace and combined with it, so that results may accrue. Otherwise the realization of universal peace by itself in the world of mankind is difficult. As the teachings of Bahá'u'lláh are combined with universal peace, they are like a table provided with every kind of fresh and delicious food. Every soul can find, at that table of infinite bounty, that which he desires. If the question is restricted to universal peace alone, the remarkable results which are expected and desired will not be attained.[33]

While universal peace is composed of myriad components, it must also guarantee all peoples the fulfillment of their highest aspirations. The salient characteristic of the Bahá'í Faith, 'Abdu'l-Bahá states, is its capacity to unite members of all races, nations, and religions, and thereby remove potential barriers to peace. He informs the Central Organization that "The scope of universal peace must be such that all the communities and religions may find their highest wish realized in it. The teachings of Bahá'u'lláh are such that all the communities of the world, whether religious, political or ethical, ancient or modern, find in them the expression of their highest wish."[34]

In discussing the application of these teachings, 'Abdu'l-Bahá demonstrates how they preserve "universal relationships."[35] Addressing the issue of the practicability of the teachings, he acknowledges that there are some teachings that, cannot, as yet, be fully carried out in the present-day circumstances. He takes as an example the institution of the Supreme Tribunal, called for by Bahá'u'lláh as part of the administrative machinery for the establishment of universal peace. He details the democratic, broadly inclusive methods by which a future Supreme Tribunal might be established, and He compares these provisions to those of a "limited and restricted" League of Nations.[36] The League of Nations, He observed, was "incapable of establishing universal peace."[37] Even so, it is important to note that He appreciated its potential—its very existence representing a serious attempt to put in place a system of collective security. 'Abdu'l-Bahá was well familiar with the ideals concerning peace enunciated by the United States President Woodrow Wilson and with his unique contribution to the creation of the League of Nations—achievements which Shoghi Effendi indicates were acclaimed by 'Abdu'l-Bahá "as signalizing the dawn of the Most Great Peace."[38]

Referring again to the experience of the Bahá'ís in Persia, 'Abdu'l-Bahá comments on their courage in the face of concerted government opposition, active persecution, death and martyrdom, and He describes how oppression and cruelty failed to hinder the spread of the teachings—such occurrences simply served to increase interest in the teachings of Bahá'u'lláh. 'Abdu'l-Bahá then informs the Executive Committee of the possibility that other people from among the Persians—who are seeking fame and fortune, who are opposed to the Bahá'í Faith, and who are intent on misrepresenting its teachings—might forward their materials to the Committee. Should this occur, He urges the Executive Committee to investigate the situation and to obtain further information from the Bahá'ís in Persia.[39]

To illustrate the potential power inherent in Bahá'u'lláh's teachings to transform individuals and build communities composed of members of many peoples, religions, and creeds, 'Abdu'l-Bahá analyzes in detail the operation of the processes of composition and decomposition or annihilation in the life of an individual, in the world of nature, and in society, and He shows how unity or composition brings strength, while division leads to social decomposition. "Whatever is the cause of harmony, attraction and union among men," He states, "is the life of the world of humanity, and whatever is the cause of difference, of repulsion and of separation is the cause of the death of mankind."[40]

Anticipating possible objections being raised about whether or not it was possible to create the kind of ideal unity and harmony envisaged in the Bahá'í teachings, 'Abdu'l-Bahá offers the following argument: "In answer we say that differences are of two kinds. One is the cause of annihilation and is like the antipathy existing among warring nations and conflicting tribes who seek each other's destruction, uprooting one another's families, depriving one another of rest and comfort and unleashing carnage, and this is blameworthy. The other kind which is a token of diversity is the essence of perfection and the cause of the appearance of divine bestowals."[41]

In developing His theme, 'Abdu'l-Bahá invites the reader to consider the flowers of a garden, with blooms of different kinds, colors and diverse forms and appearances. This diversity, He states, increases their charm, and adds unto their beauty. Likewise, "the difference of customs, manners, habits, ideas, opinions and dispositions embellishes the world of humanity, and this is praiseworthy."[42] He ascribes to the "Word of God"[43] the power to harmonize "divergent thoughts, sentiments, ideas, and convictions," concluding, "Naught but the celestial potency of the Word of God, which rules and transcends the realities of all things, is capable of harmonizing the divergent thoughts, sentiments, ideas, and convictions of the children of men. Verily, it is the penetrating power in all things, the mover of souls and the binder and regulator in the world of humanity."[44]

At the conclusion of this first Tablet to the Central Organization for a Durable Peace, 'Abdu'l-Bahá explains that He is attaching to His letter, for the information of the Organization, a copy of another Tablet concerning the universal application of the teachings of Bahá'u'lláh, which He had written during the First World War and addressed to the people of the world. When read in conjunction with the First Hague Tablet, the appended letter provides additional insights into the role of religion in society, the important contribution of individual moral priorities, and the scope of social change necessary to achieve the vision of peace set out in the Bahá'í Writings. The Tablet appears as item 1(a) in Appendix 2.

Tablet of 'Abdu'l-Bahá Appended to the First Tablet to The Hague

The appended Tablet reiterates some of the basic ideas and principles of the Bahá'í Faith. It notes, for example, that Bahá'u'lláh's teachings on unity and peace are intended to benefit the whole world and that the principle of the oneness of humankind is the cause of illumination and fellowship; and it sets out a standard of unity to which the followers of the Faith and its supporters must aspire: "Let them purify their sight and behold all humankind as leaves and blossoms and fruits of the tree of being. Let them at all times concern themselves with doing a kindly thing for one of their fellows, offering to someone love, consideration, thoughtful help. Let them see no one as their enemy, or as wishing them ill, but think of all humankind as their friends; regarding the alien as an intimate, the stranger as a companion, staying free of prejudice, drawing no lines."[45]

The Tablet employs dramatic language to contrast this high standard to the conditions of the world devoid of spiritual values and unity:

> The world is at war and the human race is in travail and mortal combat. The dark night of hate hath taken over, and the light of good faith is blotted out. The peoples and kindreds of the earth have sharpened their claws, and are hurling themselves one against the other. It is the very foundation of the human race that is being destroyed. It is thousands of households that are vagrant and dispossessed, and every year seeth thousands upon thousands of human beings weltering in their lifeblood on dusty battlefields. The tents of life and joy are down. The generals practice their generalship, boasting of the blood they shed, competing one with the next in inciting to violence. . . . On such things do men pride themselves, in such do they glory! Love—righteousness—these

are everywhere censured, while despised are harmony, and devotion to the truth.[46]

The final section of the Tablet describes the role of the religion of Bahá'u'lláh in summoning humanity to "safety and love, to amity and peace."[47] It invites the lovers of God to value "this precious Faith, obey its teachings, walk in this road that is drawn straight, and show ye this way to the people."[48] To this end they are called upon to dedicate their lives to improving "the character of each and all" and to reorienting "the minds of men," both of which are vital to achieving the "unity of conscience," referred to in the first Hague Tablet, and to putting in place the breadth of conditions necessary for the attainment of peace.[49]

The Second Tablet, Dated July 1, 1920

'Abdu'l-Bahá's second Tablet to The Hague was written in response to the Executive Committee's letter of June 12, 1920. The Tablet was translated from Persian into English in Haifa, forwarded to The Netherlands where it was translated into French, and delivered by 'Abdu'l-Bahá's representatives to members of the Executive Committee in July, 1920. The Tablet appears as item 2 in Appendix 2.

The second Hague Tablet is significantly shorter than the first. 'Abdu'l-Bahá begins by emphasizing the high regard in which Bahá'ís hold that "esteemed organization."[50] He expresses pleasure that the Bahá'ís and the organization share a vision about the importance of peace and that both have a mutual commitment to continue to work for universal peace. He addresses, at the level of principle, apparent misapprehensions expressed in the letter from the Executive Committee concerning the relevance of the multifaceted Bahá'í approach to the attainment of peace.[51]

The Tablet refers briefly to the experience of the Iranian Bahá'ís, examines the issue of peace from the perspective of personal commitment and collective action, and explores the issue of motivation and implementation—the

mobilization of people to engage in the processes of laying the foundations
of a world in which universal peace can emerge and endure.

'Abdu'l-Bahá explains to the Central Organization the centrality of peace
to the work of the Bahá'í community—where the attainment of peace is not
simply an aspiration to which they are sympathetic or a goal complementary
to their other aims. He asserts that "our desire for peace is not derived merely
from the intellect. It is a matter of religious belief and one of the eternal
foundations of the Faith of God."[52] 'Abdu'l-Bahá recalls the willingness of the
early Persian Bahá'ís to devote themselves to "the mighty cause of peace,"[53]
even in the face of persecution. Aware of their spiritual responsibility, Bahá'ís
take the long-term view and persist in their efforts to translate the spiritual
teachings into action in the promotion of peace, even when immediate results may not always be forthcoming.

The Tablet considers the ways of harnessing support for the promotion of
peace and addresses the need for "a power of implementation." 'Abdu'l-Bahá
observes that for peace to be realized in the world, it is not enough that people
should simply be informed about the horrors of war: "Today the benefits of
universal peace are recognized amongst the people, and likewise the harmful
effects of war are clear and manifest to all. But in this matter, knowledge
alone is far from sufficient. A power of implementation is needed to establish
it throughout the world."[54] He calls for consideration to be given to finding
the means to awaken the "compelling power of conscience": "Ye should therefore consider how the compelling power of conscience can be awakened, so
that this lofty ideal may be translated from the realm of thought into that of
reality. For it is clear and evident that the execution of this mighty endeavor
is impossible through ordinary human feelings but requireth the powerful
sentiments of the heart to transform its potential into reality."[55]

Recognizing the difficulty of effecting change, even in the face of agreement on a laudable course of action, 'Abdu'l-Bahá broadens the discussion by
offering the following familiar examples: "Indeed, all on earth know that an
upright character is praiseworthy and acceptable and that baseness of char-

acter is blameworthy and rejected, that justice and fairness are favored and agreeable whilst cruelty and tyranny are unacceptable and rejected. Notwithstanding this, all people, but for a few, are devoid of a praiseworthy character and bereft of a sense of justice."[56]

He acknowledges that such high aspirations cannot be attained simply by wishing for their achievement. He asserts that a spiritual force is required to motivate action and links the "power of implementation" with the "penetrating influence of the Word of God." Calling attention to the critical role of religion in the attainment of peace, He writes, "The power of conscience is therefore needed, and spiritual sentiments are required, that souls may feel compelled to evince a goodly character. It is our firm belief that the power of implementation in this great endeavor is the penetrating influence of the Word of God and the confirmations of the Holy Spirit."[57]

At the end of the Tablet, 'Abdu'l-Bahá refers once more to the warmth of the relationship between the Bahá'ís and the Executive Committee and He expresses the hope that, before long, they will witness the establishment of the oneness of the world of humanity and the emergence of universal peace. He asks the Executive Committee to continue to communicate with him and to keep him informed of the progress of universal peace in Europe.[58]

Contribution of Tablets to The Hague to the Discourse on Peace

Considered within the context of engaging in the discourses of peace, 'Abdu'l-Bahá's initiative was a step toward the involvement of the Bahá'í Faith in the discourses of society, nations, and the world at large about universal peace. The first Tablet to The Hague Committee provides a detailed discussion of the barriers to peace and the changes in conscience and consciousness necessary for its realization, while the second Tablet, which was written in response to the Committee's comments and questions arising from a reading of the first Tablet, hones in on the means for achieving the conditions necessary for the attainment of peace and offers the Bahá'í perspective on the vital role accorded to religion in inspiring and sustaining grassroots activity for the realization of peace. The pursuit of peace is, therefore, fundamentally an individual spiritual responsibility. When put into practice in daily life, spiritual and moral teachings serve as the motivating force for social action.

Together, the two Tablets offer a novel approach to the promotion of peace that is worthy of consideration. The approach articulated by 'Abdu'l-Bahá in His Tablets to The Hague is long-term and realistic. Underpinning this approach is the conviction that world peace must be built on a genuine universal framework that is inclusive of the entire human family. It requires a new level of commitment to resolving issues not customarily associated with the pursuit of peace—such as racism, the inordinate disparity between rich and poor, unbridled nationalism, religious strife, the emancipation and equality of women with men, universal education, and the adoption of an international, auxiliary language. Aimed at the prevention of war, in the long term, this approach addresses the issues of peace at the level of moral and spiritual principles—since solutions to social problems can be found through spiritual principles (human values)—and it recognizes the oneness of the human family and the role of a federated system of governance on a global scale, which will provide a means for establishing collective security. It lays the foundation for a culture of peace, where rather than investing resources in dealing with destructive conflict, resources instead are invested in recognizing and removing barriers to peace, in eliminating the causes of conflict, and in preventing the outbreak of war.

'Abdu'l-Bahá's Tablets, indeed His life's work, were focused on disseminating the contents of Bahá'u'lláh's teachings to the generality of humanity, on engaging people from all walks of life in discussions on peace, on instilling and encouraging a sense of personal commitment to the prerequisites of peace, and on imbuing a worldwide consciousness of not only the requirements but also the possibility, and inevitability, of peace. His efforts also support the discourse on the nature of the evolutionary international structures—such as the League of Nations (and the United Nations, which was not yet formed during the lifetime of 'Abdu'l-Bahá)—necessary to maintain peace.

Analysis of the Tablets to The Hague

In the final chapter, we continue the exploration of the Bahá'í perspective on peace and examine the ongoing process leading to the realization of peace.

8 / The Emergence of Peace

The Paris Peace Conference, held just over a hundred years ago in the aftermath of the ruin and suffering of World War I, embraced the need for a new world order to bring stability to the world. While the structures put in place by the assembled delegates had their limitations—and over the years proved unable to prevent repeated crises in international affairs—they represent important steps on the long journey towards real and lasting peace.

The long-term vision of peace outlined in the revelation Bahá'u'lláh and promoted by the life-time work of 'Abdu'l-Bahá entails removing barriers to peace and creating a culture of peace. It involves moving humanity toward "an age of peace—not merely a peace which rules out armed conflict, but a collective state of being, manifesting unity."[1]

As mentioned in an earlier chapter, Bahá'u'lláh makes the achievement of peace dependent on the establishment of unity and justice. Mankind's "well-being . . . peace and security," He states, "are unattainable unless and until its unity is firmly established."[2] 'Abdu'l-Bahá reiterated this important principle. In writing to The Hague Committee one hundred years ago, amidst the turbulence of world affairs, He stresses this salient truth: that the starting point both for peace and order in the world must be recognition that humanity is one people and the nations of the world one global community. In light of this reality, it follows that the complex array of relations both among nations and within them needs to be reenvisaged.

The Bahá'í conception of the way in which peace will emerge links the operation of two interrelated processes. The first is the evolution of a world consciousness, comprising an awareness of the oneness of humanity and the communities of nations. The second is the establishment of the means for instituting collective security, including the emergence of a system of federated nations, which will evolve through increasingly effective international collaboration into a form of global governance that will also further the unity of conscience. As outlined in Chapter 2, the Bahá'í teachings suggest that the long process leading to universal peace will occur in stages. The realization of such ends will undoubtedly require, among other things, several stages in the adjustment of both individual and national political attitudes.

Peace Will Come in Stages

The literature of the Bahá'í Faith contains a number of statements concerning stages in the progression of humanity toward the unity of nations and that illustrate the operation of two interrelated processes involving the emergence of a world consciousness and the formation of some form of global governance that will provide a means for establishing collective security.[3] These processes were described in Chapter 2. In brief, the first stage is the Lesser Peace, which is gradually evolving and will come about largely from the suffering and social upheavals of the contemporary world and it will involve the active efforts of individuals and nations to put an end to war. The second stage is the Most Great Peace that relates to the growth and development of the worldwide Bahá'í community, the spread of its spiritual influence, and the further evolution and maturation of the Bahá'í Administrative Order that over time is expected to lead to the future Bahá'í Commonwealth.

A highly significant milestone in this evolutionary process was the creation of the League of Nations at the Paris Peace Conference in 1919. It was based on a covenant calling for joint action by League members against an aggressor, arbitration of international disputes, reduction of armaments, and open diplomacy. As noted in an earlier chapter, the lack of political will of member states to intervene in acts of aggression by one state against another contributed to the demise of the League and rendered it powerless to prevent World War II.

A further important step toward peace and world order was taken during the Second World War and resulted in the establishment of the United Nations. Despite the problems encountered by the League of Nations in arbitrating conflict and ensuring international peace and security prior to World War II, the major Allied powers—the United States, the United Kingdom, and Soviet Russia—agreed during the war to establish a new global organization to help manage international affairs. They took the lead in designing the new organization and determining its decision-making structure and functions. In April 1945, an international conference, attended by representatives of fifty countries from all geographic areas of the world, was convened in San Francisco. The Charter of the United Nations was finalized on April 25, 1945 and signed on June 26 1945, in San Francisco, at the conclusion of the United Nations Conference on International Organization and came into force on October 24, 1945.[4]

The primary objective of the United Nations, which came into being in the aftermath of World War II, was to save future generations from the devastation of international conflict. Designed to ensure international peace and security, the new intergovernmental organization represented, in many ways, a continuum with the League of Nations. Many of the UN's principal organs and related agencies were adopted from similar structures established earlier in the century. However, in some respects, the United Nations constituted a very different organization, especially in regard to its objective of maintaining international peace and security and its commitment to economic and social development.

The aspirations of the United Nations are broad and visionary. According to the preamble of its Charter, the United Nations aims to "save succeeding generations from the scourge of war, . . . to reaffirm faith in fundamental human rights, . . . to establish conditions under which justice and respect for the obligations arising from treaties and other sources of international law can be maintained, and to promote social progress and better standards of life in larger freedom."[5]

The United Nations' main function of preserving international peace and security are set out in chapters VI and VII of the UN Charter. In brief, chapter VI provides for the pacific settlement of disputes—through the intervention of the Security Council—by means such as negotiation, mediation, arbitration, and judicial decisions.[6] Chapter VII details the provisions regarding the goal of collective security, whereby aggression against one member is met with resistance by all. Among other things, chapter VII grants the Security Council the power to order coercive measures—ranging from diplomatic, economic, and military sanctions to the use of armed force—in cases where attempts at a peaceful settlement have failed. Such measures were seldom applied during the Cold War, however, because tensions between the two super-powers prevented the Security Council from agreeing on the instigators of aggression. Instead, actions to maintain peace and security often took the form of preventive diplomacy and peacekeeping. In the post-Cold War period, appeals to the UN for peacekeeping and related activities increased dramatically, and new threats to international peace and security were confronted, including AIDS and international terrorism.[7] In 1992, the UN created the Department of Peacekeeping Operations (DPKO), which provides administrative and technical support for political and humanitarian missions and coordinates all mine-clearing activities conducted under UN auspices.[8]

The work of the United Nations has been greatly enriched by a system of international economic and humanitarian institutions that have emerged, and by advances in relation to human rights and international law. The Economic and Social Council (ECOSOC), established in chapter X of the Charter, has a special mandate in relation to human rights. The UN Charter empowered ECOSOC to establish "commissions in economic and social fields and for the promotion of human rights.[9] One of these was the United Nations Human Rights Commission, which under the chairmanship of Eleanor Roosevelt saw the creation of the Universal Declaration of Human Rights. The Declaration was drafted by representatives of all regions of the world and encompassed all legal traditions. It was formally adopted by the United Nations on December 10, 1948, and it has been described as "the most universal human rights document in existence, delineating the thirty fundamental rights that form the basis for a democratic society."[10]

The United Nations, like the League of Nations, has played a major role in defining, codifying, and expanding the realm of international law. The International Law Commission, established by the General Assembly in 1947, is the primary institution responsible for these activities. The International Court of Justice, also known as the World Court, is the principal judicial organ of the United Nations. The court's origins predate the League of Nations. Indeed the idea for the creation of an international court to arbitrate international disputes arose during an international conference held at The Hague in 1899. This institution was subsumed under the League of Nations in 1919 as the Permanent Court of International Justice (PCIJ) and adopted its present name with the founding of the United Nations in 1945.[11] The International Court of Justice reinforces legal norms through its judgments. The International Law Commission has influenced international law in several important domains, including the laws of war, the law of the sea, human rights, and international terrorism.[12]

Steps Toward the Emergence of World Mindedness and Governmental Structures

The League of Nations, the United Nations, and the many organizations and agreements produced by them have unquestionably been helpful in attenuating some of the negative effects of international conflicts, but they have, to date, shown themselves incapable of preventing war.

Both the League and the United Nations were designed to ensure international peace and security. However, inherent in the organizational structure of both institutions are a number of factors that potentially undermine the achievement of its goals. For example, in relation to the United Nations, although the world has changed dramatically—particularly with respect to the post-Cold War relationship between the United States and Russia and the dramatic increase in the number of independent states—the UN's organizational structure still reflects the power relationships of the immediate post-1945 world. Fomerand and associates observe that "The UN is a reflection of the realities of international politics, and the world's political and economic divisions are revealed in the voting arrangements of the Security Council, the blocs and cleavages of the General Assembly, the different viewpoints within the Secretariat, the divisions present at global conferences, and the financial and budgetary processes."[13] With respect to the functioning of the United Nations, Fomerand et al comment:

> Despite its intensively political nature, the UN has transformed itself and some aspects of international politics. Decolonization was successfully accomplished, and the many newly independent states joined the international community and have helped to shape a new international agenda. The UN has utilized Charter provisions to develop innovative methods to address peace and security issues. The organization has tried new approaches to economic development, encouraging the establishment of specialized organizations to meet specific needs. It has organized global conferences on urgent international issues, thereby placing new issues on the international agenda and allowing greater participation by NGOs and individuals.
>
> Notwithstanding its accomplishments, the United Nations still operates under the basic provision of respect for national sovereignty and noninterference in the domestic affairs of states. The norm of national sovereignty, however, runs into persistent conflict with the constant demand by many in the international community that the UN take a more active role in combating aggression and alleviating international problems . . . Thus it is likely that the UN will continue to be seen by its

critics as either too timid or too omnipotent as it is asked to resolve the most pressing problems faced by the world's most vulnerable citizens.[14]

While it is beyond the scope of this chapter to provide a detailed account of the activities of the United Nations, it is suggested that the United Nations represents a contribution both to the process of organizational development and to the emergence of world consciousness. For example, an important outcome of the Second World War was the willingness of national governments to create a new system of international order and to endow it with the peacekeeping authority that had been denied to the defunct League of Nations. A second breakthrough occurred with the adoption by the United Nations of the Universal Declaration of Human Rights. The moral commitment this declaration represented was institutionalized in the subsequent establishment of the United Nations Commission on Human Rights. Highlighting the significance of both advances was

... the decision of the nations that had triumphed in the recent conflict to put on trial leading figures of the Nazi regime. For the first time in history, the leaders of a sovereign nation—men who sought to argue the constitutionality of the political positions they had occupied— were brought before a public court, their crimes unsparingly reviewed and documented, were duly convicted, and those who did not escape through suicide were then either hanged or sentenced to long terms of imprisonment. No serious protest had been raised against this procedure which, theoretically, constituted a fundamental departure from existing norms of international law . . . It demonstrated, for the first time, that . . . "national sovereignty" has recognizable and enforceable limits.[15]

Paradoxically, the period following the formation of the United Nations Organization has exhibited both a growing consciousness of unity among the nations and peoples of the planet, understood as "a unity which arises from a recognition among the peoples of the various nations, that they are members of one common human family,"[16] and also a resurgence of nationalism:

> . . . a system of international economic institutions came into being, and historic advances were made relating to human rights and international law. In rapid succession, many territories under colonial rule became independent nations, and arrangements for regional cooperation grew markedly in depth and range. The post-war decades, however, were also characterized by an atmosphere of brooding and often open hostility between the world's two major power blocs. . . . [T]he Cold War . . . spilled over into actual wars in various regions of the world, and brought humanity perilously close to a conflict involving nuclear weapons.[17]

In relation to processes or trends at work in the world in the closing years of the twentieth century that potentially foreshadowed the emergence of peace, the Universal House of Justice, the international governing body of the Bahá'í Faith, called attention to the global gathering held to mark the fiftieth anniversary of the United Nations, "at which the attending heads of state and heads of government asserted their commitment to world peace."[18] The House of Justice noted "the promptitude and spontaneity with which these government leaders have been acting together in responding to a variety of crises in different parts of the world," and it linked these trends with "the increasing cries from enlightened circles for attention to be given to the feasibility of achieving some form of global governance."[19] Furthermore, writing in 1998, the Universal House of Justice identified two additional trends. The first concerned "the greater involvement of the United Nations, with the backing of powerful governments, in attending to long-standing and urgent world problems;" and the second "derives from the dramatic recognition by world leaders in only recent months of what the interconnectedness of all nations in the matter of trade and finance really implies[20]—a condition that Shoghi Effendi anticipated as an essential aspect of an organically unified world."[21]

Reviewing the significant events that occurred in the world during this period, the House of Justice stated during April (Riḍván) 2000 that "world leaders took bold steps towards fashioning the structures of a global political peace" and that ". . . attempts at implementing and elaborating the methods of collective security were earnestly made, bringing to mind one of Bahá'u'lláh's prescriptions for maintaining peace; a call was raised for an international criminal court to be established, another action that accords with Bahá'í expectations; to focus attention on the imperative need for an adequate system to deal with global issues, world leaders are scheduled to meet in a Millennium Summit; new methods of communications have opened the way for everyone to communicate with anyone on the planet."[22]

As a preliminary to the Millennium Summit, the United Nations convened a series of world conferences on themes of importance to humanity's future. These occasions provided new opportunities for collaboration and building consensus on a global scale. The "purposeful deliberative process" undertaken at these gatherings "culminated at the turn of the century in the Millennium Forum, a meeting of representatives of over a thousand civil society organizations from more than a hundred countries, followed by the Millennium Summit, an unparalleled gathering of world leaders which led to agreement on a set of objectives representing a shared ambition of humanity. Styled the Millennium Development Goals, they became rallying points for collective action in ensuing years."[23]

The Way Forward

The twentieth century was distinguished by the gradual emergence of unity of thought among nations. This movement stands in sharp contrast to the nationalistic tenor of the nineteenth century and suggests changing attitudes among the peoples of the world and their leaders. Though in some areas the progress has been marked, limitations and imperfections still persist, and conflicts continue to rage in the world. From a Bahá'í perspective, however, these advances represent "signs of a widespread, gradual but inexorable rise in global consciousness on the part of the earth's peoples and their attraction to universal justice, to solidarity, to collaboration, to compassion, and to equality."[24]

However, recent history demonstrates that the movement toward the unity among the community of nations is unpredictable and likely to be long-term. Elaborating on this theme, Shoghi Effendi, in a letter written in 1947 when the United Nations had just replaced the League of Nations and was itself proceeding along the path of development of its powers and functions, anticipated that this process of organizational development "must, however long and tortuous the way, lead, through a series of victories and reverses, to the political unification of the Eastern and Western Hemispheres, to the emergence of a world government and the establishment of the Lesser Peace, as foretold by Bahá'u'lláh and foreshadowed by the Prophet Isaiah."[25]

The twentieth century might well have ended with a glimmer of hope that the goodwill generated by agreement on the Millennium Development Goals might at last usher in a brighter, more peaceful future for all humankind. However, the challenges encountered in the early years of the twenty-first century appear to have interrupted this process. Instead of drawing people together, many of the dominant currents in societies everywhere seem to be pushing people apart, breeding a decline in public trust, and fueling fundamental instability in world affairs. Commenting on the impact of this trend, the House of Justice observes, "the will to engage in international collective action, which twenty years ago represented a powerful strain of thinking among world leaders, has been cowed, assailed by resurgent forces of racism, nationalism, and factionalism."[26]

The will to engage in collective action in the pursuit of peace, and to rise above narrow self-interest will, doubtless, require several stages in the adjustment of national political attitudes. For the present, the United Nations does not possess such a mandate, nor is there anything in the current discourse of political leaders that seriously envisions so radical a restructuring of the administration of the affairs of the planet. Commenting on the current situation, the Universal House of Justice places progress toward peace within an historical and spiritual context, writing, "Universal peace is the destination towards which humanity has been moving throughout the ages under the influence of the Word of God that has been progressively imparted by the Creator to His creation." It refers to Shoghi Effendi's description of humanity's advance towards a new, global stage in its collective life in terms of social evolution and underlines the present priority: "A global order that unifies the nations with the assent of humanity is the only adequate answer to the destabilizing forces that threaten the world."[27]

Little by Little—Day by Day

Much remains to be done before the age of peace envisioned in the Bahá'í teachings becomes a reality. The establishment of peace is a duty to which the entire human race is called. Peace begins with each individual, and it must be consciously and methodically built.

We have seen in this volume how 'Abdu'l-Bahá dedicated His life to promoting a culture of peace. While still a youth, He wrote to the leaders and people of Persia, the land of His birth, encouraging them to work for the revitalization of their once-great country, which had fallen into social and economic decline during the Qájár dynasty. He suggested the following course of action for socially responsible individuals: "We must now highly resolve to arise and lay hold of all those instrumentalities that promote the peace and well-being and happiness, the knowledge, culture and industry, the dignity, value and station, of the entire human race. Thus, through the restoring waters of pure intention and unselfish effort, the earth of human potentialities will blossom with its own latent excellence and flower into praiseworthy qualities, and bear and flourish until it comes to rival that rose garden of knowledge which belonged to our forefathers."[28]

A World Without War

He persisted in His service while a prisoner of the Ottoman Empire, and despite age and failing health, He set out in 1911 on a momentous journey to the West to disseminate the teachings of Bahá'u'lláh, to raise public awareness, and to mobilize support for peace including through His participation at the historic Lake Mohonk Conference. With the outbreak of World War I, just months after His return to the Holy Land, He dedicated His time to humanitarian activities to alleviate the hunger and suffering of the local population. As the conflict ground inexorably on, 'Abdu'l-Bahá—anxious to ensure the worldwide promotion of peace—wrote fourteen historic letters to His followers in North America. Known collectively as the Tablets of the Divine Plan, these letters are considered to be the charter for the worldwide spread of the Bahá'í Faith and its values of unity, peace, and justice. They resonated with the hunger for peace which characterized the mood of the period and set in motion processes—both within the Bahá'í community and beyond—designed to lay the foundation for universal peace and to bring about the spiritual transformation of the planet. And in the aftermath of the Great War, 'Abdu'l-Bahá addressed several letters to the Executive Committee of the Central Organization for a Durable Peace at The Hague detailing the Bahá'í viewpoint on peace and highlighting the importance of mobilizing the power of implementation.

The teachings of Bahá'u'lláh set out a broad framework for a new way of life for humanity, a way of life that promotes a universal consciousness and enables the establishment of a peaceful and united society. For a Bahá'í, the ultimate issues are spiritual. A statement, commissioned by the Universal House of Justice, highlights the role of the individual in laying the foundations for peace and the approach taken in exercising his or her personal responsibility: "The Cause is not a political party nor an ideology, much less an engine for political agitation against this or that social wrong. The process of transformation it has set in motion advances by inducing a fundamental change of consciousness, and the challenge it poses to everyone who would serve it is to free oneself from attachment to inherited assumptions and preferences that are irreconcilable with the Will of God for humanity's coming of age."[29]

Today, there is a continuing urgent need for the international community to actively work to create an environment in which a sustainable peace can emerge. In the Tablets to The Hague, 'Abdu'l-Bahá stressed the importance of identifying ways to mobilize action—to harness the power of implementation. What can be done to foster increased understanding of the significance of the principle of the oneness of humankind and its implications for social interactions and international governmental relations? Are there effective steps that might be taken to realize the ideals in the Universal Declaration of Human Rights and its related covenants and to address the challenging issues facing humanity at the present moment in its history? What can be done to learn from and support diverse peace initiatives around the world?

The timing and nature of the historical forces that will eventually precipitate widespread acceptance of the principle of world government and convince national governments and other centers of power to willingly cede sufficient authority to create an effective and just international federal system are currently unknown. Nevertheless, are there steps that might be taken now to become informed about proposals for changes in international governmental structures, to participate in discussions about changes to the international order, to support the movement for peace, and to prepare the ground for the transition from the present system of national sovereignty to a system of world government?

Much can be learned from the life of 'Abdu'l-Bahá, from His Writings and talks, His engagement in discourses on peace, and from the contents of His seminal Tablets to the Executive Committee of the Central Organization for a Durable Peace at The Hague. Witness His wide and continual dissemination of the subject of peace, His engagement in discussions of peace with people from all walks of life, and the ways in which He instilled and encouraged a sense of personal commitment to the prerequisites of peace. Consider also how He described the high degree of unity achieved, a hundred years ago, among the Bahá'ís in Iran, and how He offered this as an example of the power of Bahá'u'lláh's teachings to motivate individuals to strive to remove barriers to a peaceful society and to imbue populations with hope. 'Abdu'l-Bahá mentioned how the Bahá'ís of Iran came from varied religious backgrounds, including Zoroastrians, Christians, Jews, and Muslims. How extraordinary it was that, despite the deep tensions and conflicts that existed among the diverse religions in Iran and the active hostility of the ruling class toward the Bahá'í community, the spiritual principles and ideas put forth in the Bahá'í teachings changed the hearts of its new adherents and removed obstacles to division and dissension among the Bahá'ís of Iran.

'Abdu'l-Bahá's discourses on peace offered a far-reaching spiritual vision and understanding of the means by which the possibility of a peaceful world becomes achievable. To whomever He spoke and in whatever setting, His example and words were inclusive of all the members of the human family, and they realistically expressed the complex and multilayered process leading to peace and called on every individual, religious or not, to become engaged in actions that unite people toward expanding human understanding, uplifting human conditions, and advancing the process toward the establishment of universal peace:

> In cycles gone by, though harmony was established, yet, owing to the absence of means, the unity of all mankind could not have been achieved. Continents remained widely divided, nay even among the peoples of one and the same continent association and interchange of thought were wellnigh impossible. Consequently intercourse, understanding and unity amongst all the peoples and kindreds of the earth were unattainable. In this day, however, means of communication have multiplied, and the five continents of the earth have virtually merged into one. . . . In like manner all the members of the human family, whether peoples or governments, cities or villages, have become increasingly interdependent. For none is self-sufficiency any longer possible,

inasmuch as political ties unite all peoples and nations, and the bonds of trade and industry, of agriculture and education, are being strengthened every day. Hence the unity of all mankind can in this day be achieved.[30]

"Small steps, if they are regular and rapid, add up to a great distance travelled."[31]

'Abdu'l-Bahá in the Holy Land, c. 1920. Photo credit: Bahá'í Media Bank.
https://media.bahai.org/history/images-related-central-figures/abdul-baha/.

'Abdu'l-Bahá at Stanford University Palo Alto, CA.
Photo credit: U.S. Bahá'í National Center Archives.

Lake Mohonk Mountain House, New Paltz, NY. Left to Right: E.C.
Getsinger, Lua Getsinger, Valíyu'lláh Varqá, Amín Fareed, Aḥmad Sohráb,
'Abdu'l-Bahá, Siyyid Asadu'lláh, Zíá Baghdádí.Photo credit: U.S. Bahá'í
National Center Archives.

'Abdu'l-Bahá receiving knighthood for relief of distress and famine during World War I, April 27, 1920. Photo credit: Bahá'í Media Bank.

Ibn-i-Aṣdaq, Hand of the Cause of God.
Photo credit: Bahá'í World News Service.
https://news.bahai.org/story/1378/slideshow/3/.

Aḥmad Yazdání. Photo credit: Yazdání family photo.

Appendix 1 / Address of 'Abdu'l-Bahá to Lake Mohonk Conference on May 15, 1912

May 15, 1912[1]

SECOND SESSION – Lake Mohonk Conference on International Arbitration Wednesday Evening, May 15, 1912

THE CHAIRMAN: I am sure we are all glad to cordially welcome as the first speaker this evening 'ABDU'L-BAHA ABBAS, of Persia, the well-known leader of the Bahá'í movement.

THE ONENESS OF THE REALITY OF HUMANKIND

ADDRESS OF 'ABDU'L-BAHÁ ABBAS

When we consider history, we find that civilization is progressing, but in this century its progress cannot be compared with that of past centuries. This is the century of light and of bounty. In the past, the unity of patriotism, the unity of nations and religions was established; but in this century, the oneness of the world of humanity is established; hence this century is greater than the past.

Sixty years ago Asia was in great turmoil of wars; England, Russia, Turkey and France went to war. There were wars in Persia, wars among the religions and wars between nations, especially in Persia on account of the existence of the different nationalities, such as Turks, Persians, Arabs and Kurds, and the various religions, namely, Mohammedan, Jewish, Christian and Zoroastrian. Among these different religions the greatest enmity and rancor were extant.

At such a time as this, His Holiness, Bahá'u'lláh appeared. He proclaimed the oneness of the world of humanity and the greatest peace. He wrote to all the kings and addressed epistles to all the religionists of Persia, and all the souls who accepted his platform and emulated and followed his teachings—whether Christians, Mohammedans, Jews or Zoroastrians—were united and attained the greatest amity and unity. Through those teachings, the Kurd, the Arab, the Persian and the Turk freed themselves from the prejudice of race and were people agreed to an extent which is indescribable, indeed, in such a manner, that were you to enter their meeting you could not distinguish between the Persian, the Christian, the Arab or the Turk, and you would not observe any differences of religious opinion. Among those people the utmost of love and oneness of peace now obtain, for the great teachings of Bahá'u'lláh make for the oneness of the world and for humanity, universal peace and arbitration. The following are a few of the principles of Bahá'u'lláh.

First, that all must investigate reality. It is incumbent on all nations to investigate truth. For Bahá'u'lláh declares that the foundations of the divine religion are one and that one is reality and reality is not multiple but indivisible. But the imitations which have come in, being different in character, have caused divisions and separations. If we forsake the imitations and revert to the original foundations of the divine religion, we shall find that the foundations are that reality which is one and not multiple.

The second principle of Bahá'u'lláh is the oneness of human kind. All humanity belongs to one family, inhabiting the same globe; all are beneath the providence of God, God has created all and has nurtured all and provideth for all and preserveth all. This is the policy of God. God is kind to all and why should we be unkind? Is there any policy wiser and better than God's policy? No matter how keen the human mind may be, it cannot surpass the policy of God. The policy of God is perfect and we must follow it and not our own self-interest.

The third teaching of Bahá'u'lláh is that religion and science are twins. If a religious question be not in accordance with science, it is imagination. All religious matter must correspond with science, every question which meets the criterion of science shall be acceptable, and those questions which do not come to the standard of science are not to be given credence. The fourth teaching of Bahá'u'lláh is that religion should be the one bond which shall unite society, which shall cement together the various peoples, which shall cause a unity among all the creeds. If religion should be productive of strife and division, if it should cause bloodshed and war and rapine, irreligion is preferable to religion. Religion was meant to be a bond of love among mankind.

The fifth principle is that racial bias, religious prejudice, patriotic prejudice, political prejudice, are the destroyers of the very foundations of the body politic. All humanity is one in kind, the surface of the earth one home, and the foundations of the divine religions one. All the wars which have taken place since the inception of human history have emanated either from religious prejudice, racial prejudice, patriotic bias or political greed and interest. As long as these prejudices last, so long will the foundations of humanity tremble. When such prejudices pass away the world will at last find peace.

The sixth principle of Bahá'u'lláh is equality between mankind and womankind. Woman and man are both human and both the manifestations of God's grace. God has created man and has endowed him with knowledge and intelligence. The difference which now exists between man and woman is only a difference of education, and when woman shall receive the same education no doubt her equality with man shall become a reality. The world of humanity is composed of two organizations—the male and the female. If one organ be defective, that defect will affect the other. Until perfect strength shall obtain in both, and woman shall attain equality with man, the happiness of humanity will not be insured.

Appendix 1

The seventh principle concerns the readjustment of the economic questions in the social body. The rich now enjoy the greatest luxury, whereas the poor are in abject misery. Certain laws must be made whereby the rich cannot become over-rich and the poor shall not starve, both rich and poor enjoying the comforts according to their respective deserts.

The eighth principle of Bahá'u'lláh is that philosophy sufficeth not and is not conducive to the absolute happiness of mankind. Great philosophers have been capable of educating themselves, or a few who followed them, but generally education, ethical education, they could not endow. Therefore, the world of humanity is evermore in need of the breath of the Holy Spirit. The greatest peace will not be realized without the power of the Holy Spirit. It is the Holy Spirit of God which insures the safety of humanity, for human thoughts differ, human susceptibilities differ. You cannot make the susceptibilities of all humanity one except through the common channel of the Holy Spirit.

(Report of the Eighth Annual Lake Mohonk Conference on International Arbitration, May 15–17, 1912, pp. 42–44)

Appendix 2 / Tablets to The Hague

Item 1

First Tablet to The Hague[1]

17 December 1919

O YE esteemed ones who are pioneers among the well-wishers of the world of humanity!

The letters which ye sent during the war were not received, but a letter dated February 11th, 1916, has just come to hand, and immediately an answer is being written. Your intention deserves a thousand praises, because you are serving the world of humanity, and this is conducive to the happiness and welfare of all. This recent war has proved to the world and the people that war is destruction while universal peace is construction; war is death while peace is life; war is rapacity and bloodthirstiness while peace is beneficence and humaneness; war is an appurtenance of the world of nature while peace is of the foundation of the religion of God; war is darkness upon darkness while peace is heavenly light; war is the destroyer of the edifice of mankind while peace is the everlasting life of the world of humanity; war is like a devouring wolf while peace is like the angels of heaven; war is the struggle for existence while peace is mutual aid and cooperation among the peoples of the world and the cause of the good pleasure of the True One in the heavenly realm.

There is not one soul whose conscience does not testify that in this day there is no more important matter in the world than that of universal peace. Every just one bears witness to this and adores that esteemed Assembly because its aim is that this darkness may be changed into light, this bloodthirstiness into kindness, this torment into bliss, this hardship into ease and this enmity and hatred into fellowship and love. Therefore, the effort of those esteemed souls is worthy of praise and commendation.

But the wise souls who are aware of the essential relationships emanating from the realities of things consider that one single matter cannot, by itself, influence the human reality as it ought and should, for until the minds of men become united, no important matter can be accomplished. At present universal peace is a matter of great importance, but unity of conscience is essential, so that the foundation of this matter may become secure, its establishment firm and its edifice strong.

Therefore Bahá'u'lláh, fifty years ago, expounded this question of universal peace at a time when He was confined in the fortress of 'Akká and was wronged and imprisoned. He wrote about this important matter of universal peace to all the great sovereigns of the world, and established it among His friends in the Orient. The horizon of the East was in utter darkness, nations displayed the utmost hatred and enmity towards each other, religions thirsted for each other's blood, and it was darkness upon darkness. At such a time Bahá'u'lláh shone forth like the sun from the horizon of the east and illumined Persia with the lights of these teachings.

Among His teachings was the declaration of universal peace. People of different nations, religions and sects who followed Him came together to such an extent that remarkable gatherings were instituted consisting of the various nations and religions of the East. Every soul who entered these gatherings saw but one nation, one teaching, one pathway, one order, for the teachings of Bahá'u'lláh were not limited to the establishment of universal peace. They embraced many teachings which supplemented and supported that of universal peace.

Among these teachings was the independent investigation of reality so that the world of humanity may be saved from the darkness of imitation and attain to the truth; may tear off and cast away this ragged and outgrown garment of a thousand years ago and may put on the robe woven in the utmost purity and holiness in the loom of reality. As reality is one and cannot admit of multiplicity, therefore different opinions must ultimately become fused into one.

And among the teachings of Bahá'u'lláh is the oneness of the world of humanity; that all human beings are the sheep of God and He is the kind Shepherd. This Shepherd is kind to all the sheep, because He created them all, trained them, provided for them and protected them. There is no doubt that the Shepherd is kind to all the sheep and should there be among these sheep ignorant ones, they must be educated; if there be children, they must be trained until they reach maturity; if there be sick ones, they must be cured. There must be no hatred and enmity, for as by a kind physician these ignorant, sick ones should be treated.

And among the teachings of Bahá'u'lláh is that religion must be the cause of fellowship and love. If it becomes the cause of estrangement then it is not needed, for religion is like a remedy; if it aggravates the disease then it becomes unnecessary.

And among the teachings of Bahá'u'lláh is that religion must be in conformity with science and reason, so that it may influence the hearts of men. The foundation must be solid and must not consist of imitations.

And among the teachings of Bahá'u'lláh is that religious, racial, political, economic and patriotic prejudices destroy the edifice of humanity. As long as these prejudices prevail, the world of humanity will not have rest. For a period of 6,000 years history informs us about the world of humanity. During these 6,000 years the world of humanity has not been free from war, strife, murder and bloodthirstiness. In every period war has been waged in one country or another and that war was due to either religious prejudice, racial prejudice, political prejudice or patriotic prejudice. It has therefore been ascertained and proved that all prejudices are destructive of the human edifice. As long as these prejudices persist, the struggle for existence must remain dominant, and bloodthirstiness and rapacity continue. Therefore, even as was the case in the past, the world of humanity cannot be saved from the darkness of nature and cannot attain illumination except through the abandonment of prejudices and the acquisition of the morals of the Kingdom.

If this prejudice and enmity are on account of religion consider that religion should be the cause of fellowship, otherwise it is fruitless. And if this prejudice be the prejudice of nationality consider that all mankind are of one nation; all have sprung from the tree of Adam, and Adam is the root of the tree. That tree is one and all these nations are like branches, while the individuals of humanity are like leaves, blossoms and fruits thereof. Then the establishment of various nations and the consequent shedding of blood and destruction of the edifice of humanity result from human ignorance and selfish motives.

As to the patriotic prejudice, this is also due to absolute ignorance, for the surface of the earth is one native land. Every one can live in any spot on the terrestrial globe. Therefore all the world is man's birthplace. These boundaries and outlets have been devised by man. In the creation, such boundaries and outlets were not assigned. Europe is one continent, Asia is one continent, Africa is one continent, Australia is one continent, but some of the souls, from personal motives and selfish interests, have divided each one of these continents and considered a certain part as their own country. God has set up no frontier between France and Germany; they are continuous. Yet, in the first centuries, selfish souls, for the promotion of their own interests, have assigned boundaries and outlets and have, day by day, attached more importance to these, until this led to intense enmity, bloodshed and rapacity in subsequent centuries. In the same way this will continue indefinitely, and if this conception of patriotism remains limited within a certain circle, it will be the primary cause of the world's destruction. No wise and just person will acknowledge these imaginary distinctions. Every limited area which we call our native country we regard as our motherland, whereas the terrestrial globe is the motherland of all, and not any restricted area. In short, for a few days we live on this earth and eventually we are buried in it, it is our eternal tomb. Is it worth while that we should engage in bloodshed and tear one another to pieces for this eternal tomb? Nay, far from it, neither is God pleased with such conduct nor would any sane man approve of it.

Consider! The blessed animals engage in no patriotic quarrels. They are in the utmost fellowship with one another and live together in harmony. For example, if a dove from the east and a dove from the west, a dove from the north and a dove from the south chance to arrive, at the same time, in one spot, they immediately associate in harmony. So is it with all the blessed animals and birds. But the ferocious animals, as soon as they meet, attack and fight with each other, tear each other to pieces and it is impossible for them to live peaceably together in one spot. They are all unsociable and fierce, savage and combative fighters.

Regarding the economic prejudice, it is apparent that whenever the ties between nations become strengthened and the exchange of commodities accelerated, and any economic principle is established in one country, it will ultimately affect the other countries and universal benefits will result. Then why this prejudice?

As to the political prejudice, the policy of God must be followed and it is indisputable that the policy of God is greater than human policy. We must follow the Divine policy and that applies alike to all individuals. He treats all individuals alike: no distinction is made, and that is the foundation of the Divine Religions.

And among the teachings of Bahá'u'lláh is the origination of one language that may be spread universally among the people. This teaching was revealed from the pen of Bahá'u'lláh in order that this universal language may eliminate misunderstandings from among mankind.

And among the teachings of Bahá'u'lláh is the equality of women and men. The world of humanity has two wings—one is women and the other men. Not until both wings are equally developed can the bird fly. Should one wing remain weak, flight is impossible. Not until the world of women becomes equal to the world of men in the acquisition of virtues and perfections, can success and prosperity be attained as they ought to be.

And among the teachings of Bahá'u'lláh is voluntary sharing of one's property with others among mankind. This voluntary sharing is greater than equality, and consists in this, that man should not prefer himself to others, but rather should sacrifice his life and property for others. But this should not be introduced by coercion so that it becomes a law and man is compelled to follow it. Nay, rather, man should voluntarily and of his own choice sacrifice his property and life for others, and spend willingly for the poor, just as is done in Persia among the Bahá'ís.

And among the teachings of Bahá'u'lláh is man's freedom, that through the ideal Power he should be free and emancipated from the captivity of the world of nature; for as long as man is captive to nature he is a ferocious animal, as the struggle for existence is one of the exigencies of the world of nature. This matter of the struggle for existence is the fountain-head of all calamities and is the supreme affliction.

And among the teachings of Bahá'u'lláh is that religion is a mighty bulwark. If the edifice of religion shakes and totters, commotion and chaos will ensue and the order of things will be utterly upset, for in the world of mankind there are two safeguards that protect man from wrongdoing. One is the law which punishes the criminal; but the law prevents only the manifest crime and not the concealed sin; whereas the ideal safeguard, namely, the religion of God, prevents both the manifest and the concealed crime, trains man, educates morals, compels the adoption of virtues and is the all-inclusive power which guarantees the felicity of the world of mankind. But by religion is meant that which is ascertained by investigation and not that which is based on mere imitation, the foundations of Divine Religions and not human imitations.

And among the teachings of Bahá'u'lláh is that although material civilization is one of the means for the progress of the world of mankind, yet until it becomes combined with Divine civilization, the desired result, which is the felicity of mankind, will not be attained. Consider! These battleships that reduce a city to ruins within the space of an hour are the result of material civilization; likewise the Krupp guns, the Mauser rifles, dynamite, submarines, torpedo boats, armed aircraft and bombers—all these weapons of war are the malignant fruits of material civilization. Had material civilization been combined with Divine civilization, these fiery weapons would never have been invented. Nay, rather, human energy would have been wholly devoted to useful inventions and would have been concentrated on praiseworthy discoveries. Material civilization is like a lamp-glass. Divine civilization is the lamp itself and the glass without the light is dark. Material civilization is like the body. No matter how infinitely graceful, elegant and beautiful it may be, it is dead. Divine civilization is like the spirit, and the body gets its life from the spirit, otherwise it becomes a corpse. It has thus been made evident that the world of mankind is in need of the breaths of the Holy Spirit. Without the spirit the world of mankind is lifeless, and without this light the world of mankind is in utter darkness. For the world of nature is an animal world. Until man is born again from the world of nature, that is to say, becomes detached from the world of nature, he is essentially an animal, and it is the teachings of God which convert this animal into a human soul.

And among the teachings of Bahá'u'lláh is the promotion of education. Every child must be instructed in sciences as much as is necessary. If the parents are able to provide the expenses of this education, it is well, otherwise the community must provide the means for the teaching of that child.

And among the teachings of Bahá'u'lláh are justice and right. Until these are realized on the plane of existence, all things shall be in disorder and remain imperfect. The world of mankind is a world of oppression and cruelty, and a realm of aggression and error.

In fine, such teachings are numerous. These manifold principles, which constitute the greatest basis for the felicity of mankind and are of the bounties of the Merciful, must be added to the matter of universal peace and combined with it, so that results may accrue. Otherwise the realization of universal peace by itself in the world of mankind is difficult. As the teachings of Bahá'u'lláh are combined with universal peace, they are like a table provided with every kind of fresh and delicious food. Every soul can find, at that table of infinite bounty, that which he desires. If the question is restricted to universal peace alone, the remarkable results which are expected and desired will not be attained. The scope of universal peace must be such that all the communities and religions may find their highest wish realized in it. The teachings of Bahá'u'lláh are such that all the communities of the world, whether religious, political or ethical, ancient or modern, find in them the expression of their highest wish.

For example, the people of religions find, in the teachings of Bahá'u'lláh, the establishment of Universal Religion—a religion that perfectly conforms with present conditions, which in reality effects the immediate cure of the incurable disease, which relieves every pain, and bestows the infallible antidote for every deadly poison. For if we wish to arrange and organize the world of mankind in accordance with the present religious imitations and thereby to establish the felicity of the world of mankind, it is impossible and impracticable—for example, the enforcement of the laws of the Torah and also of the other religions in accordance with present imitations. But the essential basis of all the Divine Religions which pertains to the virtues of the world of mankind and is the foundation of the welfare of the world of man, is found in the teachings of Bahá'u'lláh in the most perfect presentation.

Similarly, with regard to the peoples who clamour for freedom: the moderate freedom which guarantees the welfare of the world of mankind and maintains and preserves the universal relationships, is found in its fullest power and extension in the teachings of Bahá'u'lláh.

So with regard to political parties: that which is the greatest policy directing the world of mankind, nay, rather, the Divine policy, is found in the teachings of Bahá'u'lláh.

Likewise with regard to the party of "equality" which seeks the solution of the economic problems: until now all proposed solutions have proved impracticable except the economic proposals in the teachings of Bahá'u'lláh which are practicable and cause no distress to society.

So with the other parties: when ye look deeply into this matter, ye will discover that the highest aims of those parties are found in the teachings of Bahá'u'lláh. These teachings constitute the all-inclusive power among all men and are practicable. But there are some teachings of the past, such as those of the Torah, which cannot be carried out at the present day. It is the same with the other religions and the tenets of the various sects and the different parties.

For example, the question of universal peace, about which Bahá'u'lláh says that the Supreme Tribunal must be established: although the League of Nations has been brought into existence, yet it is incapable of establishing universal peace. But the Supreme Tribunal which Bahá'u'lláh has described will fulfil this sacred task with the utmost might and power. And His plan is this: that the national assemblies of each country and nation—that is to say parliaments—should elect two or three persons who are the choicest of that nation, and are well informed concerning international laws and the relations between governments and aware of the essential needs of the world of humanity in this day. The number of these representatives should be in proportion to the number of inhabitants of that country. The election of these souls who are chosen by the national assembly, that is, the parliament, must be confirmed by the upper house, the congress and the cabinet and also by the president or monarch so these persons may be the elected ones of all the nation and the government. The Supreme Tribunal will be composed of these people, and all mankind will thus have a share therein, for every one of these delegates is fully representative of his nation. When the Supreme Tribunal gives a ruling on any international question, either unanimously or by majority rule, there will no longer be any pretext for the plaintiff or ground of objection for the defendant. In case any of the governments or nations, in the execution of the irrefutable decision of the Supreme Tribunal, be negligent or dilatory, the rest of the nations will rise up against it, because all the governments and nations of the world are the supporters of this Supreme Tribunal. Consider what a firm foundation this is! But by a limited and restricted League the purpose will not be realized as it ought and should. This is the truth about the situation, which has been stated.

Consider how powerful are the teachings of Bahá'u'lláh. At a time when He was in the prison of 'Akká and was under the restrictions and threats of two bloodthirsty kings, His teachings, notwithstanding this fact, spread with all power in Persia and other countries. Should any teaching, or any principle, or any community fall under the threat of a powerful and bloodthirsty monarch, it would be annihilated within a short space of time. At present and for fifty years the Bahá'ís in Persia and most regions have been under severe restrictions and the threat of sword and spear. Thousands of souls have given their lives in the arena of sacrifice and have fallen as victims under the swords of oppression and cruelty. Thousands of esteemed families have been uprooted and destroyed. Thousands of children have been made fatherless. Thousands of fathers have been bereft of their sons. Thousands of mothers have wept and lamented for their boys who have been beheaded. All this oppression and cruelty, rapacity and bloodthirstiness did not hinder or prevent the spread of the teachings of Bahá'u'lláh. They spread more and more every day, and their power and might became more evident.

It may be that some foolish person among the Persians will affix his name to the contents of the Tablets of Bahá'u'lláh or to the explanations given in the letters of 'Abdu'l-Bahá and send it to that esteemed Assembly. Ye must be aware of this fact, for any Persian who seeks fame or has some other intention will take the entire contents of the Tablets of Bahá'u'lláh and publish them in his own name or in that of his community, just as happened at the Universal Races Congress in London before the war. A Persian took the substance of the Epistles of Bahá'u'lláh, entered that Congress, gave them forth in his own name and published them, whereas the wording was exactly that of Bahá'u'lláh. Some such souls have gone to Europe and have caused confusion in the minds of the people of Europe and have disturbed the thoughts of some Orientalists. Ye must bear this fact in mind, for not a word of these teachings was heard in Persia before the appearance of Bahá'u'lláh. Investigate this matter so that it may become to you evident and manifest. Some souls are like parrots. They learn any note which they may hear, and sing it, but they themselves are unaware of what they utter. There is a sect in Persia at present made up of a few souls who are called Bábís, who claim to be followers of the Báb, whereas they are utterly unaware of Him. They have some secret teachings which are entirely opposed to the teachings of Bahá'u'lláh and in Persia people know this. But when these souls come to Europe, they conceal their own teachings and utter those of Bahá'u'lláh, for they know that the teachings of Bahá'u'lláh are powerful and they therefore declare publicly those teachings of Bahá'u'lláh in their own name. As to their secret teachings, they say that they are taken from the Bayán and the Bayán is from the Báb. When ye obtain the translation of the Bayán, which has been translated in Persia, ye will discover the truth that the teachings of Bahá'u'lláh are utterly opposed to the teachings of this sect. Beware lest ye disregard this fact. Should ye desire to investigate the matter further, enquire from Persia.

In brief, when you traverse the regions of the world, thou shalt conclude that all progress is the result of association and co-operation, while ruin is the outcome of animosity and hatred. Notwithstanding this, the world of humanity does not take warning, nor does it awake from the slumber of heedlessness. Man is still causing differences, quarrels and strife in order to marshal the cohorts of war and, with his legions, rush into the field of bloodshed and slaughter.

Appendix 2

Then again, consider the phenomenon of composition and decomposition, of existence and non-existence. Every created thing in the contingent world is made up of many and varied atoms, and its existence is dependent on the composition of these. In other words, a conjunction of simple elements takes place so that from this composition a distinct organism is produced. The existence of all things is based upon this principle. But when the order is deranged, decomposition is produced and disintegration sets in, then that thing ceases to exist. That is, the annihilation of all things is caused by decomposition and disintegration. Therefore attraction and composition between the various elements is the means of life, and discord, and division produce death. Thus the cohesive and attractive forces in all things lead to the appearance of fruitful results and effects, while estrangement and alienation of things lead to disturbance and annihilation. Through affinity and attraction all living things like plants, animals and men come into existence, while division and discord bring about decomposition and destruction.

Consequently, that which is conducive to association and attraction and unity among the sons of men is the means of the life of the world of humanity, and whatever causes division, repulsion and remoteness leads to the death of humankind.

And if, as you pass by fields and plantations, where the plants, flowers and sweet-smelling herbs are growing luxuriantly together, forming a pattern of unity, this is an evidence of the fact that that plantation and garden is flourishing under the care of a skilful gardener. But when you see it in a state of disorder and irregularity you infer that it has lacked the training of an efficient farmer and thus has produced weeds and tares.

It therefore becomes manifest that amity and cohesion are indicative of the training of the Real Educator, and dispersion and separation a proof of savagery and deprivation of divine education.

A critic may object, saying that peoples, races, tribes and communities of the world are of different and varied customs, habits, tastes, character, inclinations and ideas, that opinions and thoughts are contrary to one another, and how, therefore, is it possible for real unity to be revealed and perfect accord among human souls to exist?

In answer we say that differences are of two kinds. One is the cause of annihilation and is like the antipathy existing among warring nations and conflicting tribes who seek each other's destruction, uprooting one another's families, depriving one another of rest and comfort and unleashing carnage, and this is blameworthy. The other kind which is a token of diversity is the essence of perfection and the cause of the appearance of divine bestowals.

Consider the flowers of a garden: though differing in kind, colour, form and shape, yet, inasmuch as they are refreshed by the waters of one spring, revived by the breath of one wind, invigorated by the rays of one sun, this diversity increases their charm, and adds unto their beauty. Thus when that unifying force, the penetrating influence of the Word of God, takes effect, the difference of customs, manners, habits, ideas, opinions and dispositions embellishes the world of humanity, and this is praiseworthy. This diversity, this difference is like the naturally created dissimilarity and variety of the limbs and organs of the human body, for each one contributes to the beauty, efficiency and perfection of the whole. When these different limbs and organs come under the influence of man's sovereign soul, and the soul's power pervades the limbs and members, veins and arteries of the body, then difference reinforces harmony, diversity strengthens love, and multiplicity is the greatest factor for co-ordination.

How unpleasing to the eye if all the flowers and plants, the leaves and blossoms, the fruits, the branches and the trees of that garden were all of the same shape and colour! Diversity of hues, form and shape, enriches and adorns the garden, and heightens the effect thereof. In like manner, when divers shades of thought, temperament and character, are brought together under the power and influence of one central agency, the beauty and glory of human perfection will be revealed and made manifest. Naught but the celestial potency of the Word of God, which rules and transcends the realities of all things, is capable of harmonizing the divergent thoughts, sentiments, ideas, and convictions of the children of men. Verily, it is the penetrating power in all things, the mover of souls and the binder and regulator in the world of humanity.

Praise be to God, today the splendour of the Word of God has illumined every horizon, and from all sects, races, tribes, nations, and communities souls have come together in the light of one Word, assembled, united and agreed in perfect harmony.

Some time ago, during the war, a letter was written regarding the teachings of Bahá'u'lláh which may appropriately be appended to this epistle.

Item 1(a)

Appended Tablet[2]

O PEOPLES of the world! The Sun of Truth hath risen to illumine the whole earth, and to spiritualize the community of man. Laudable are the results and the fruits thereof, abundant the holy evidences deriving from this grace. This is mercy unalloyed and purest bounty; it is light for the world and all its peoples; it is harmony and fellowship, and love and solidarity; indeed it is compassion and unity, and the end of foreignness; it is the being at one, in complete dignity and freedom, with all on earth.

The Blessed Beauty saith: "Ye are all the fruits of one tree, the leaves of one branch." Thus hath He likened this world of being to a single tree, and all its peoples to the leaves thereof, and the blossoms and fruits. It is needful for the bough to blossom, and leaf and fruit to flourish, and upon the interconnection of all parts of the world-tree, dependeth the flourishing of leaf and blossom, and the sweetness of the fruit.

For this reason must all human beings powerfully sustain one another and seek for everlasting life; and for this reason must the lovers of God in this contingent world become the mercies and the blessings sent forth by that clement King of the seen and unseen realms. Let them purify their sight and behold all humankind as leaves and blossoms and fruits of the tree of being. Let them at all times concern themselves with doing a kindly thing for one of their fellows, offering to someone love, consideration, thoughtful help. Let them see no one as their enemy, or as wishing them ill, but think of all humankind as their friends; regarding the alien as an intimate, the stranger as a companion, staying free of prejudice, drawing no lines.

In this day, the one favoured at the Threshold of the Lord is he who handeth round the cup of faithfulness; who bestoweth, even upon his enemies, the jewel of bounty, and lendeth, even to his fallen oppressor, a helping hand; it is he who will, even to the fiercest of his foes, be a loving friend. These are the Teachings of the Blessed Beauty, these the counsels of the Most Great Name.

O ye dear friends! The world is at war and the human race is in travail and mortal combat. The dark night of hate hath taken over, and the light of good faith is blotted out. The peoples and kindreds of the earth have sharpened their claws, and are hurling themselves one against the other. It is the very foundation of the human race that is being destroyed. It is thousands of households that are vagrant and dispossessed, and every year seeth thousands upon thousands of human beings weltering in their lifeblood on dusty battlefields. The tents of life and joy are down. The generals practice their generalship, boasting of the blood they shed, competing one with the next in inciting to violence. "With this sword," saith one of them, "I beheaded a people!" And another: "I toppled a nation to the ground!" And yet another: "I brought a government down!" On such things do men pride themselves, in such do they glory! Love—righteousness—these are everywhere censured, while despised are harmony, and devotion to the truth.

The Faith of the Blessed Beauty is summoning mankind to safety and love, to amity and peace; it hath raised up its tabernacle on the heights of the earth, and directeth its call to all nations. Wherefore, O ye who are God's lovers, know ye the value of this precious Faith, obey its teachings, walk in this road that is drawn straight, and show ye this way to the people. Lift up your voices and sing out the song of the Kingdom. Spread far and wide the precepts and counsels of the loving Lord, so that this world will change into another world, and this darksome earth will be flooded with light, and the dead body of mankind will arise and live; so that every soul will ask for immortality, through the holy breaths of God.

Soon will your swiftly passing days be over, and the fame and riches, the comforts, the joys provided by this rubbish-heap, the world, will be gone without a trace. Summon ye, then, the people to God, and invite humanity to follow the example of the Company on high. Be ye loving fathers to the orphan, and a refuge to the helpless, and a treasury for the poor, and a cure for the ailing. Be ye the helpers of every victim of oppression, the patrons of the disadvantaged. Think ye at all times of rendering some service to every member of the human race. Pay ye no heed to aversion and rejection, to disdain, hostility, injustice: act ye in the opposite way. Be ye sincerely kind, not in appearance only. Let each one of God's loved ones centre his attention on this: to be the Lord's mercy to man; to be the Lord's grace. Let him do some good to every person whose path he crosseth, and be of some benefit to him. Let him improve the character of each and all, and reorient the minds of men. In this way, the light of divine guidance will shine forth, and the blessings of God will cradle all mankind: for love is light, no matter in what abode it dwelleth; and hate is darkness, no matter where it may make its nest. O friends of God! That the hidden Mystery may stand revealed, and the secret essence of all things may be disclosed, strive ye to banish that darkness for ever and ever.

Item 2

Second Tablet to The Hague[3]

1 July 1920

Appendix 2

TO THE esteemed members of the Executive Committee of the Central Organization for a Durable Peace

Your reply, dated 12 June 1920, to my letter was received with the utmost gratitude. God be praised, it testified to the unity of thought and purpose that existeth between us and you, and expressed sentiments of the heart that bear the hallmark of sincere affection.

We Bahá'ís have the greatest affinity for your esteemed organization, and dispatched therefore two distinguished individuals to you in order to forge a strong bond. For in this day the cause of universal peace is of paramount importance amongst all human affairs and is the greatest instrument for securing the very life and felicity of mankind. Bereft of this effulgent reality, humanity can in no wise find true composure or real advancement but will, day by day, sink ever deeper into misery and wretchedness.

This last terrible war hath clearly proven that humanity cannot withstand the effects of modern instruments of warfare. The future can in no wise be compared to the past, for earlier weapons and armaments had but a feeble effect, whilst modern ones can, in a brief span of time, strike at the very roots of the world of humanity and surpass the limits of its endurance.

In this age, therefore, universal peace is like unto the sun, which bestoweth life upon all things, and it is thus incumbent upon all to endeavour in the path of this mighty cause. Now, we indeed share this common goal with you and strive toward it with all our strength, renouncing even our lives, our kindred, and our substance for its sake.

As ye have no doubt heard, in Persia thousands of souls have offered up their lives in this path, and thousands of homes have been laid waste. Despite this, we have in no wise relented, but have continued to endeavour unto this very moment and are increasing our efforts as day followeth day, because our desire for peace is not derived merely from the intellect: It is a matter of religious belief and one of the eternal foundations of the Faith of God. That is why we strive with all our might and, forsaking our own advantage, rest, and comfort, forgo the pursuit of our own affairs; devote ourselves to the mighty cause of peace; and consider it to be the very foundation of the Divine religions, a service to His Kingdom, the source of eternal life, and the greatest means of admittance into the heavenly realm.

Today the benefits of universal peace are recognized amongst the people, and likewise the harmful effects of war are clear and manifest to all. But in this matter, knowledge alone is far from sufficient: A power of implementation is needed to establish it throughout the world. Ye should therefore consider how the compelling power of conscience can be awakened, so that this lofty ideal may be translated from the realm of thought into that of reality. For it is clear and evident that the execution of this mighty endeavour is impossible through ordinary human feelings but requireth the powerful sentiments of the heart to transform its potential into reality.

Indeed, all on earth know that an upright character is praiseworthy and acceptable and that baseness of character is blameworthy and rejected, that justice and fairness are favoured and agreeable whilst cruelty and tyranny are unacceptable and rejected. Notwithstanding this, all people, but for a few, are devoid of a praiseworthy character and bereft of a sense of justice.

The power of conscience is therefore needed, and spiritual sentiments are required, that souls may feel compelled to evince a goodly character. It is our firm belief that the power of implementation in this great endeavour is the penetrating influence of the Word of God and the confirmations of the Holy Spirit.

We are bound to you by the strongest ties of love and unity. We long with heart and soul for the day to arrive when the tabernacle of the oneness of humanity will have been raised in the midmost heart of the world and the banner of universal peace unfurled in all regions. The oneness of humanity must therefore be established, that the edifice of universal peace may be raised in turn.

Your organization, which is a well-wisher of the world of humanity, is highly esteemed in the eyes of the Bahá'ís. Therefore kindly accept our highest regards and keep us ever informed of the progress of the cause of universal peace in Europe through your efforts. We hope that our communications will remain constant.

Notes

1 / Enlarging the Framework for Peace

1. See, for example, Strachan, *The First World War*.
2. Strachan, *The First World War*, p. xxv.
3. In recent years, the Universal House of Justice, the international governing council of the Bahá'í Faith, has encouraged the world-wide Bahá'í community to engage in the "discourses of society (April 27, 2017)." A large number of Bahá'í principles and ideas directly address current social issues such as global governance, the equality of women, eradication of racism, inequality, human rights, climate change and ecology, and the like. Bahá'ís are encouraged to contribute to public discourse where general Bahá'í principles are put forth to assist in advancing thinking and policies regarding various social problems. The purpose of discourse is not to win converts. Rather, by engaging in discourse Bahá'ís hope to contribute possible ideas and solutions to the betterment of society (see the letters of the Universal House of Justice dated Riḍván 2010 to the Bahá'ís of the World, and April 27, 2017 to an individual).
4. Universal House of Justice, letter dated January 18, 2019 to the Bahá'ís of the World. https://www.bahai.org/library/authoritative-texts/the-universal-house-of-justice/messages/20190118_001/1#963030050.
5. Bahá'u'lláh, *Gleanings from the Writings of Bahá'u'lláh*, no. 106.1.
6. The Universal House of Justice, letter dated January 18, 2019 to the Bahá'ís of the World. https://www.bahai.org/library/authoritative-texts/the-universal-house-of-justice/messages/20190118_001/1#963030050.

Notes

2 / The Bahá'í Faith and Peace:
Principles of an Integrated, Holistic Peace

1. The Universal House of Justice, message dated January 18, 2019 addressed to the Bahá'ís of the World, paragraph 1.
2. Shoghi Effendi, "The Faith of Bahá'u'lláh, A World Religion," *World Order*, vol. XIII, no. 7 (October, 1947): 2.
3. Hoda Mahmoudi, "Human Knowledge and the Advancement of Society," *The Journal of Bahá'í Studies*, vol. 22, no. 1–4 (2012): 69–87.
4. Bahá'í International Community. *Who is Writing the Future?* New York: Bahá'í International Community, 1999.
5. Bahá'u'lláh, *Gleanings from the Writings of Bahá'u'lláh*, no. 27.5.
6. Ibid., no. 109.2.
7. Ibid., no. 31.1.
8. Ibid., no. 34.5. See Robert N. Bellah, *Religion in Human Evolution: From the Paleolithic to the Axial Age*. Cambridge, MA: The Belknap Press of Harvard University Press, 2011; S. N. Eisenstadt, "The Axial Age Breakthroughs—Their Characteristics and Origins," in *The Origins and Diversity of the Axial Age*, ed. S. N. Eisenstadt. Albany: SUNY Press, 1986.
9. Bahá'u'lláh, *Gleanings from the Writings of Bahá'u'lláh*, no. 34.5.
10. Ibid., no. 31.1.
11. Bahá'u'lláh, The Kitáb-i-Aqdas: The Most Holy Book, ¶182.
12. Bahá'u'lláh, *Tablets of Bahá'u'lláh Revealed after the Kitáb-i-Aqdas*, p. 129.
13. Ibid., p. 129.
14. See statement of 'Abdu'l-Bahá, cited in The Universal House of Justice, letter dated March 2, 2013 to the Bahá'ís of Iran, paragraph 15.
15. Bahá'u'lláh, *Gleanings from the Writings of Bahá'u'lláh*, 132.2.
16. Ibid., no. 34.5.
17. Shoghi Effendi, *The World Order of Bahá'u'lláh*, p. 43.
18. Bahá'u'lláh, *The Summons of the Lord of Hosts*, "Súriy-i-Mulúk," no. 8.
19. Bahá'u'lláh, Epistle to the Son of the Wolf, p. 30.
20. Ibid.
21. Bahá'u'lláh, *The Summons of the Lord of Hosts*, "Súriy-i-Mulúk," no. 8.
22. Ibid., "Súriy-i-Haykal," no. 182.
23. Bahá'u'lláh, *Gleanings from the Writings of Bahá'u'lláh*, no. 131.2.
24. Bahá'u'lláh, *Tablets of Bahá'u'lláh Revealed after the The Kitáb-i-Aqdas*, p. 165.
25. Bahá'u'lláh, *Gleanings from the Writings of Bahá'u'lláh*, no. 119.5.
26. Shoghi Effendi, *The World Order of Bahá'u'lláh*, p. 202.
27. Zürn, *A Theory of Global Governance: Authority, Legitimacy, and Contestations*, p. 107.
28. Ibid.
29. Ibid., p. 36.

30. Ibid.; also see N. Krisch, *Beyond Constitutionalism: The Pluralist Structure of Post-national Law*.
31. See B. Mazlish and A. Iriye (eds), *The Global History Reader*. Abingdon: Routledge, 2005; M. Nussbaum, *For Love of Country: Debating the Limits of Patriotism*. Boston, MA: Beacon Press, 1996; D. Held, *Democracy and the Global Order: From the Modern State to Global Governance*. Cambridge: Polity Press, 1995.
32. The Universal House of Justice, "Introduction," in Bahá'u'lláh, Kitáb-i-Aqdas: The Most Holy Book, p. 11.
33. Shoghi Effendi, *The World Order of Bahá'u'lláh*, pp. 41–42.
34. Bahá'u'lláh, *Gleanings from the Writings of Bahá'u'lláh*, no. 131.2.
35. Ibid., no. 4.2.
36. Ibid., no. 70.1.
37. Shoghi Effendi, *The World Order of Bahá'u'lláh*, p. 144.
38. For details of the community-building activities undertaken by the Bahá'í community, refer to http://www.bahai.org.
39. The Universal House of Justice, Message dated March 2, 2013 to the Bahá'ís of Iran, p. 6.
40. 'Abdu'l-Bahá, *Paris Talks: Addresses Given by 'Abdu'l-Bahá in 1911*, no. 45.3.
41. Bahá'u'lláh, *Gleanings from the Writings of Bahá'u'lláh*, no. 110.1.
42. Bahá'u'lláh, *Epistle to the Son of the Wolf*, pp. 26–27.
43. 'Abdu'l-Bahá, *The Promulgation of Universal Peace: Talks Delivered by 'Abdu'l-Bahá during His Visit to the United States and Canada in 1912*, p. 244.
44. Ibid., p. 148.
45. Shoghi Effendi, *The World Order of Bahá'u'lláh*, pp. 41–42.
46. For a summary of Bahá'u'lláh's vision of the future World Order, see an extract from a letter dated March 11, 1936 written by Shoghi Effendi in *The World Order of Bahá'u'lláh*, pp. 203–4.
47. From a letter dated February 8, 1934 written by Shoghi Effendi, in *The World Order of Bahá'u'lláh*, p. 144.
48. From a letter dated March 21, 1930 written by Shoghi Effendi in *The World Order of Bahá'u'lláh*, p. 19.
49. William S. Hatcher & J. Douglas Martin, *The Bahá'í Faith: The Emerging Global Religion*, pp. 142–43.
50. From a letter dated June 5, 1947, written by Shoghi Effendi in *Citadel of Faith: Messages to America, 1947–1957*, p. 38.
51. From a letter dated March 11, 1936 written by Shoghi Effendi in *The World Order of Bahá'u'lláh*, pp. 162–63.
52. For additional reading about the worldwide Bahá'í community's action for peace, see The Universal House of Justice, letter dated January 18, 2019 to the Bahá'ís of the World, paragraph 11:

They cultivate environments in which children can be raised untainted by any form of racial, national, or religious prejudice. They champion the full equality of women with men in the affairs of the community. Their programmes of education, transformative in their effects and encompassing both the material and spiritual aspects of life, welcome everyone who wishes to contribute to the community's prosperity. In the stirrings of social action can be seen their desire to remedy the numerous ills afflicting humanity and to empower each person to become a protagonist in the building of a new world. Taking inspiration from the concept of the Mashriqu'l-Adhkár [Dawning-place of the Praises or "Remembrances" of God], they invite to their devotional meetings followers of all faiths and none. Youth, distinguished for their commitment to a society founded on peace and justice, are engaging their like-minded peers in the work of building communities on this foundation. In the institution of the Local Spiritual Assembly exists the spiritual authority and the administrative capacity to govern in servitude, to resolve conflicts, and to build unity; the electoral process through which Assemblies are formed is itself an expression of peace, in contrast to the vitriol and even violence that often accompanies elections in the wider society. Implicit in all these dimensions of an open, expanding community is the foundational recognition that all of humanity are the children of one Creator (Universal House of Justice, letter dated January 18, 2019 to the Bahá'ís of the World).

53. Cited in *'Abdu'l-Bahá in Canada*, p. 51.

3 / Signs of the Times—Historical Context for War and Peace

1. Bahá'u'lláh, *Gleanings from the Writings of Bahá'u'lláh*, no. 106.1.
2. McEvedy, *The Century World History Factfinder*, p. 120.
3. From Lukacs, *Remembered Past: A Reader*, p. ix.
4. Tuchman, *The Proud Tower: A Portrait of the World Before the War, 1890–1914*, p. xiii.
5. Nicolson, *The Perfect Summer: England 1911, Just Before the Storm* p. 15.
6. Tuchman, *The Proud Tower: A Portrait of the World Before the War, 1890–1914*, p. xiv.
7. Ibid.
8. Material based on chapters in Esmond Wright (Gen. Ed.), *History of the World, the Last Five Hundred Years*; https://en.wikipedia.org/wiki/History_of_Asia; http://courses.wcupa.edu/jones/his312/lectures/19thcent.htm.
9. Hobsbawm, *The Age of Empire: 1875–1914*, p. 13.
10. Ferguson, *The War of the World: History's Age of Hatred*, p. 5.
11. Blom, *The Vertigo Years: Europe, 1900–1914*, p. 86.

12. Tuchman, *The Proud Tower: A Portrait of the World Before the War, 1890–1914*, p. 270.
13. Nicolson, *The Perfect Summer: England 1911, Just Before the Storm*, p. 38
14. Hobsbawm, *The Age of Empire: 1875–1914*, p. 243.
15. Wolke, "Marie Curie's Doctoral Thesis: Prelude to a Nobel Prize," *Journal of Chemical Education*, vol. 65, no. 7 (July 1988): 561–73.
16. Blom, *The Vertigo Years: Europe, 1900–1914*, p. 86.
17. Center for the History of Medicine. "Sir Francis Galton." https://collections. countway.harvard.edu/onview/exhibits/show/galtonschildren/sir-francis-galton
18. For a detailed discussion, see Phillip Blom, *The Vertigo Years: Europe, 1900–1914*, pp. 334–59.
19. Koller, "Nationalism and Racism in Franco-German Controversies about Colonial Soldiers." In Nico Wouters and Laurence van Ypersele (eds.), *Nations, Identities and the First World War: Shifting Loyalties to the Fatherland.*, pp. 213–32. See Lauren, *Power and Prejudice: The Politics and Diplomacy of Racial Discrimination*, pp. 75–81.
20. Ibid., p. 218.
21. Fogarty, "Race, racism, and military strategy" (http://www.bl.uk/world-war-one/articles/race-racism-and-military-strategy), and "Contract workers in World War One" (http://www.bl.uk/world-war-one/articles/contract-workers-in-world-war-one), World War One web site, the British Library, January 2014.
22. Saul Friedländer, *The Years of Extermination: Nazi Germany and the Jews, 1939–1945*, p. 14.
23. Blom, *The Vertigo Years: Europe, 1900–1914*, p. 281.
24. Ibid.
25. Waldemar Januszczak (writer and director), *Gaugin: The Full Story* (video), 2003.
26. Hodgkinson, "Culture quake: The Post Impressionist exhibition," British Library. https://www.bl.uk/20th-century-literature/articles/culture-quake-the-post-impressionist-exhibition-1910.
27. Blom, *The Vertigo Years: Europe, 1900–1914*, p. 63.
28. Ibid., p. 190.
29. Hobsbawm, p. 201.
30. Blom, *The Vertigo Years: Europe, 1900–1914*, p. 2.
31. W. E. B. Du Bois, *The Souls of Black Folk*, New York: Penguin 1903, pp. 1–2.
32. Tuchman, *The Proud Tower: A Portrait of the World Before the War, 1890–1914*, p. 64.
33. Samuel R. Williamson, Jr., "The Way to War." https://encyclopedia.1914-1918-online.net/article/the_way_to_war. Accessed August 26, 2019.
34. A. J. P. Taylor, cited in "Western Europe." http://www.historyhome.co.uk/europe/causeww1.htm. Accessed August 26, 2019.

35. Niall Ferguson, *The War of the World: History's Age of Hatred*, p. 73.
36. Ibid., p. 73. The six heads of states assassinated at the time were President Carnot of France in 1894, Premier Canovas of Spain in 1897, Empress Elizabeth of Austria in 1898, King Humbert of Italy in 1900, President McKinley of the United States in 1901, and another premier in Spain—José Canalejas y Méndez—in 1912 (refer to Barbara Tuchman, *The Proud Tower: A Portrait of the World Before the War, 1890–1914*, p. 63).
37. Tuchman, *The Proud Tower: A Portrait of the World Before the War, 1890–1914*, p. 63.
38. Tonge, "A Web of English History," Causes of the First World War. http://www.historyhome.co.uk/europe/causeww1.htm.
39. Kissinger, *World Order*, p. 82.
40. H. G. Wells, *A Short History of the World*, p. 307.
41. For details, refer to A.W. Palmer, *A Dictionary of Modern History 1789–1945*, p. 354.
42. H. G. Wells, *A Short History of the World*, p. 307.
43. For additional details, see *Century of Light* pp. 33–35.
44. Hobsbawm, "Barbarism: A User's Guide," in *On History*, pp. 256–57.
45. Royde-Smith, "World War I." https://www.britannica.com/event/World-War-I#ref53113.

4 / Movements toward Peace

1. Doty, *The Central Organisation for A Durable Peace (1915–1919), Its History, Work and Ideas*, pp. 7–8.
2. Ibid, pp. 8–9.
3. Cohen, "Fighting for Peace Amid Paralyzed Popular Opinion: Bertha von Suttner's and Rosa Mayreder's Pacifist-Feminist Insights on Gender, War and Peace," in Bruna Bianchi and Geraldine Ludbrook, eds. *Living War, Thinking Peace (1914–1924): Women's Experiences, Feminist Thought, and International Relations*, p. 115.
4. Blom, *The Vertigo Years, Europe 1900–1914*, p. 192.
5. Ibid., p. 192.
6. Studies of the pre-1914 movement in Europe include Cooper, Sandi: *Patriotic Pacifism. Waging War on War in Europe, 1815–1914* (New York 1991); and essays by Roger Chickering, Jost Dülffer, Solomon Wank, and Werner Simon in Chatfield, Charles and van den Dungen, Peter (eds.): *Peace Movements and Political Cultures*, pp. 3–80. Brief biographies of almost all the individual peace advocates mentioned in this essay are in Josephson, Harold et al (eds.): *Biographical Dictionary of Modern Peace Leaders*.
7. For details of the 1899 Peace Conference at The Hague see, James L. Tryon,

"The Hague Conferences," *The Yale Law Journal,* vol. 20, no. 6 (April, 1911): 473. https://www.jstor.org/stable/784505. Accessed July 10, 2018. For the texts of the Conventions and the Final Act of the 1899 and 1907 Conferences, see A Pearce Higgins, *The Hague Peace Conferences, and other International Conferences concerning the Laws and Usages of War* (Cambridge: University Press, 1909).

8. For details, see http://opil.ouplaw.com/view/10.1093/law:epil/9780199231690/law-9780199231690-e05, paragraph 9.

9. Cited in Doty, *The Central Organisation for A Durable Peace (1915–1919), Its History, Work and Ideas,* p. 11.

10. Ibid., pp. 11–12.

11. The countries represented were Austria-Hungary, Belgium, Bulgaria, China, Denmark, France, Germany, Greece, Italy, Japan, Luxemburg, Mexico, Montenegro, the Netherlands, Persia, Portugal, Romania, Russia, Serbia, Siam, Spain, Sweden and Norway, Switzerland, Turkey, the United Kingdom of Great Britain and Ireland, and the United States of America. "Peace conference at The Hague 1899, General Report of the United States Commission," July 31, 1899. http://avalon.law.yale.edu/19th_century/hag99-04.asp.

12. Tryon, "The Hague Conferences," *The Yale Law Journal,* vol. 20, no. 6 (April, 1911): 470–485). https://www.jstor.org/stable/784505. Accessed September 10, 2018.

13. Tuchman, in *The Proud Tower, A Portrait of the World Before the War, 1890–1914,* p. 255.

14. Tryon, "The Hague Conferences," *The Yale Law Journal,* vol. 20. no 6 (April, 1911): 470–85. https://www.jstor.org/stable/784505. Accessed September 10, 2018.

15. Ibid., p. 471 and p. 472.

16. "Hague Appeal for Peace." https://thehaguepeace.org. Accessed November 26, 2017.

17. James L. Tryon, "The Hague Conferences," *The Yale Law Journal,* vol. 20, no. 6 (April 1911), p. 473. https://www.jstor.org/stable/784505. Accessed July 10, 2018.

18. "Peace Conference at the Hague 1899: Russian Circular January 11, 1899 (December 30, 1898, Old Style." http://avalon.law.yale.edu/19th_century/hag99-02.asp.

19. A. Pearce Higgins, *The Hague Peace Conferences, and other International Conferences concerning the Laws and Usages of War,* pp. 42–48.

20. Baker, "Hague Peace Conferences (1899 and 1907). http://opil.ouplaw.com/view/10.1093/law:epil/9780199231690/law-9780199231690-e305, paras.13–19.

21. Higgins, *The Hague Peace Conferences, and other International Conferences concerning the Laws and Usages of War,* pp. 42–48.

22. Doty, *The Central Organisation for A Durable Peace (1915–1919), Its History, Work and Ideas,* pp. 14–15.
23. Tuchman, *The Proud Tower, A Portrait of the World Before the War, 1890–1914,* p. 298.
24. Higgins, *The Hague Peace Conferences, and other International Conferences concerning the Laws and Usages of War,* p. 10.
25. For details of the 1899 Peace Conference at The Hague, see Tryon, "The Hague Conferences," *The Yale Law Journal,* vol. 20, no. 6 (April, 1911): 473. https://www.jstor.org/stable/784505. Accessed July 10, 2018. For the texts of the Conventions and the Final Act of the 1899 and 1907 Conferences, see A Pearce Higgins, *The Hague Peace Conferences, and other International Conferences concerning the Laws and Usages of War.*
26. Hayashi, *The Role and Importance of the Hague Conferences: A Historical Perspective,* UNIDIR 2017, p. 3.
27. For the texts of the Conventions and the Final Act of the 1899 and 1907 Conferences, see A Pearce Higgins, *The Hague Peace Conferences, and other International Conferences concerning the Laws and Usages of War.*
28. Tryon, "The Hague Conferences," *The Yale Law Journal,* vol. 20, no. 6 (April, 1911): 485. https://www.jstor.org/stable/784505. Accessed 07-10-2018.
29. Doty, *The Central Organisation for A Durable Peace (1915–1919), Its History, Work and Ideas,* p. 21.
30. Patterson, David S.: Pacifism, in: 1914-1918-online. *International Encyclopedia of the First World War,* ed. by Ute Daniel, Peter Gatrell, Oliver Janz, Heather Jones, Jennifer Keene, Alan Kramer, and Bill Nasson, issued by Freie Universität Berlin. Berlin October 8, 2014. DOI: 10.15463/ie1418.10125., p. 3.
31. Ibid., p. 7.
32. Russell, *The Autobiography of Bertrand Russell,* pp. 52–53.
33. Winter, "How the Great War Shaped the World." https://www.theatlantic.com/magazine/archive/2014/08/how-the-great-war-shaped-the-world/373468/. Special commemorative issue of *The Atlantic* on WWI.
34. Quoted in Patterson, *Search for Negotiated Peace,* p. 240.
35. Einstein, cited in Patterson, David S.: "Pacifism," in: 1914-1918-online. *International Encyclopedia of the First World War,* ed. by Ute Daniel, Peter Gatrell, Oliver Janz, Heather Jones, Jennifer Keene, Alan Kramer, and Bill Nasson, issued by Freie Universität Berlin, Berlin October 8, 2014. DOI: 10.15463/ie1418.10125., p. 8.
36. Patterson, David S.: "Pacifism," in: 1914-1918-online. *International Encyclopedia of the First World War,* ed. by Ute Daniel, Peter Gatrell, Oliver Janz, Heather Jones, Jennifer Keene, Alan Kramer, and Bill Nasson, issued by Freie Universität Berlin, Berlin October 8, 2014. DOI: 10.15463/ie1418.10125., p. 14.
37. Wikipedia, "Hague Conventions of 1899 and 1907." https://en.wikipedia.org/wiki/Hague_Conventions_of_1899_and_1907. Accessed May 11, 2018.

38. Doty, *The Central Organisation for A Durable Peace (1915–1919), Its History, Work and Ideas*, p. 28.
39. Ibid., pp. 27–28.
40. Cited in ibid., p. 30.
41. Ibid., pp. 29–31.
42. Ibid., p. 33.
43. Ibid., pp. 33–42. See names and details of delegates.
44. "Mysterious Hague Meeting: Not to End Present War, but to Prevent Future Ones," *The New York Times*, April 12, 1915. https://www.nytimes.com/1915/04/12/archives/mysterious-hague-meeting-not-to-end-present-war-but-to-prevent.html.
45. "The Central Organization for a Durable Peace." Author(s): Fannie Fern Andrews. Source: *The Annals of the American Academy of Political and Social Science*, Vol. 66, *Preparedness and America's International Program* (Jul., 1916), pp. 16–21. Published by: Sage Publications, Inc. in association with the American Academy of Political and Social Science Stable URL: https://www.jstor.org/stable/1013420. Accessed: 1December 19, 2018, 05:59 UTC.
46. Doty, p. 43.
47. "The Central Organization for a Durable Peace." Author(s): Fannie Fern Andrews Source: *The Annals of the American Academy of Political and Social Science*, Vol. 66, *Preparedness and America's International Program* (Jul., 1916), p. 17.
48. Cited in, Doty, *The Central Organisation for A Durable Peace (1915–1919), Its History, Work and Ideas*, p. 176.
49. "The Central Organization for a Durable Peace." Author(s): Fannie Fern Andrews Source: *The Annals of the American Academy of Political and Social Science*, vol. 66, *Preparedness and America's International Program*, pp. 20–21.
50. Ibid., p. 18.
51. Ibid., p. 19.
52. Dickinson, G. Lowes, *Problems of the International Settlement*, pp. vii.
53. Doty, *The Central Organisation for A Durable Peace (1915–1919), Its History, Work and Ideas*, p. 80.
54. Ibid., pp. 32–33.
55. Patterson, David S.: "Pacifism," in: 1914-1918-online. *International Encyclopedia of the First World War*, ed. by Ute Daniel, Peter Gatrell, Oliver Janz, Heather Jones, Jennifer Keene, Alan Kramer, and Bill Nasson, issued by Freie Universität Berlin, Berlin October 8, 2014. DOI: 10.15463/ie1418.10125., p. 11.
56. Following return to America, the Women's Political Party became the Women's International League for Peace and Freedom (WILPF), with Jane Addams as president.
57. From the warring nations, only Russian and French women were absent. They either could not get passports or objected to mediation while German troops

occupied their countries, but fifty-seven French women signed a resolution endorsing the congress and regretting their absence. Belgian and German delegates expressed friendship for one another, although one Belgian delegate, fearful of becoming a subject of another country, cried out, "[J]e suis Belge avant tout." ["I am Belgian, before anything else."] Quoted in Patterson, *Search for Negotiated Peace*, p. 79.

58. Ibid., p. 12.
59. Letters of Susan I. Moody at the United States National Bahá'í Archives.
60. Patterson, David S.: "Pacifism," in: 1914–1918-online. *International Encyclopedia of the First World War*, ed. by Ute Daniel, Peter Gatrell, Oliver Janz, Heather Jones, Jennifer Keene, Alan Kramer, and Bill Nasson, issued by Freie Universität Berlin, Berlin October 8, 2014. DOI: 10.15463/ie1418.10125., p. 11.
61. Doty, *The Central Organisation for A Durable Peace (1915–1919), Its History, Work and Ideas*, p. 159.
62. Wehberg, Hans. "Die Organisation der Staatengemeinschaft." https://www.nomos-elibrary.de/10.5771/9783845210445/hans-wehberg-1885-1962, December 31, 2018.
63. Doty, *The Central Organisation for A Durable Peace (1915–1919), Its History, Work and Ideas*, pp. 159–60.
64. Ibid., p. 160.
65. Ibid., pp. 162–63 for names.
66. Ibid., pp. 163–64.
67. Ibid., p. 166.
68. "Hague Appeal for Peace." https://thehaguepeace.org. Accessed November 26, 2017.
69. Ibid.
70. Cited in ibid.
71. Following the cessation of hostilities in 1918, peace activists of the Great War era continued to work energetically for peace. Indeed, peace movements exerted an important influence in the politics and diplomacy of the 1920s and 1930s. The pervasive popular disillusionment with the Great War, together with growing fears of another world war stimulated a strong, renewed interest in peace.

5 / 'Abdu'l-Bahá's Contribution to Peace
1. Bahá'u'lláh, *Gleanings from the Writings of Bahá'u'lláh*, no. 106.1.
2. Ibid.
3. 'Abdu'l-Bahá, *Selections from the Writings of 'Abdu'l-Bahá*, no. 77.1.
4. 'Abdu'l-Bahá, *The Promulgation of Universal Peace: Talks Delivered by 'Abdu'l-Bahá during His Visit to the United States and Canada in 1912*, p. 527.
5. Ibid., p. 134.

6. Ibid, p. 396.
7. Ibid., p. 492.
8. Ibid., p. 501.
9. Ibid, pp. 500–501.
10. Ibid., p. 451.
11. *'Abdu'l-Bahá in Canada*, p. 51.
12. 'Abdu'l-Bahá, Second Tablet to The Hague. See Appendix 2.
13. Ibid.
14. 'Abdu'l-Bahá, *The Secret of Divine Civilization*. Wilmette, IL: Bahá'í Publishing Trust, 1990.
15. The Universal House of Justice, November 26, 2003, letter dated November 26, 2003 to the Followers of Bahá'u'lláh in the Cradle of the Faith.
16. 'Abdu'l-Bahá, *The Secret of Divine Civilization*. ¶114.
17. Ibid., ¶171.
18. The Universal House of Justice, Riḍván 2011 letter, p. 2.
19. Ibid., p. 2.
20. Baroness von Suttner, "Hague Appeal for Peace," cited in http://www.thehague-peace.org. Accessed November 26, 2017.
21. For a detailed treatment of the reports of 'Abdu'l-Bahá's travels, see Amín Egea, *The Apostle of Peace, A Survey of References to 'Abdu'l-Bahá in the Western Press, 1971–1921*, volume One: 1871–1912 (Oxford: George Ronald): 2017.
22. 'Abdu'l-Bahá met Andrew Carnegie, possibly in Washington D.C. (Shoghi Effendi, *God Passes By*, p. 458). Both attended and spoke at the Lake Mohonk Conference (http://centenary.bahai.us/, newspaper report, May 11, 1912). When, due to illness, Carnegie was unable to attend the Master's lecture at the New York Peace Society, Mr. Short, Carnegie's friend, issued an invitation on Carnegie's behalf to 'Abdu'l-Bahá to visit Carnegie in his home (*Star of the West*, vol. III, no. 7 (13 July 1912, p. 5)). It is not clear where the meeting took place, or if they met more than once.
23. 'Abdu'l-Bahá, Tablet addressed to Andrew Carnegie, translated May 1, 1915, *Star of the West*, vol. 6, no. 11, pp. 82–83.
24. Quoted in Amín Egea, *The Apostle of Peace, A Survey of References to 'Abdu'l-Bahá in the Western Press, 1971–1921*, p. 302.
25. This correspondence was started after Mason Remey and other Bahá'ís established contact with both Smiley and Phillips at the Third National Peace Congress held in Baltimore in May 1911 where Remey presented a paper on the Bahá'í Faith. At least two Bahá'ís attended the 1911 Lake Mohonk Peace Conference: Alí-Kulí Khán, Chargé d'Affaires of the Persian Legation in the United States, gave a presentation in one of the plenary sessions on the subject of "The Conditions of Universal Peace"; Aḥmad Sohráb attended as representative of

the Persian-American Educational Society. See note 12 in Amín Egea, *The Apostle of Peace, A Survey of References to 'Abdu'l-Bahá in the Western Press, 1971–1921*, volume One: 1871–1912, p. 635.

26. Ibid., pp. 302–3.
27. Ibid., pp. 306–7.
28. Ibid., notes 19–29, p. 637.
29. See Appendix 1.
30. Ibid.
31. Ibid.
32. *Mahmud's Diary*, pp. 63–64; *Star of the West* II, Dec. 12, 1911, pp. 3–5; "'Abdu'l-Bahá In New York," *NY State Bulletin*, Part 5 & 6.
33. Shoghi Effendi, *God Passes By*, p. 482. For a detailed description refer to H.M. Balyuzi, *'Abdu'l-Bahá, The Centre of the Covenant* (Oxford: George Ronald, 1987), Chapter 22 and Lady Blomfield, *The Chosen Highway* (Wilmette: Bahá'í Publishing Trust, n.d.): Part III, Chapter 4.
34. H. M. Balyuzi, *'Abdu'l-Bahá, The Centre of the Covenant*, p. 443; for details see also Chapter 22.
35. Bahá'u'lláh, *Gleanings from the Writings of Bahá'u'lláh*, no. 4.2; *The Proclamation of Bahá'u'lláh*, p. 112.
36. Bahá'u'lláh, *The Summons of the Lord of Hosts*, (Wilmette: Bahá'í Publishing, 2006).
37. For details refer to Shoghi Effendi, *The Promised Day is Come* (Wilmette: Bahá'í Publishing Trust, 1980).
38. Shoghi Effendi, *God Passes By*, p. 483.
39. Shoghi Effendi, *Messages to the Bahá'í World, 1950–1957*, p. 35.
40. Shoghi Effendi. *God Passes By*, p. 631.
41. Amin Banani, Foreword to 'Abdu'l-Bahá, *Tablets of the Divine Plan*, p. xxi.
42. Ibid.
43. Commenting on the outcome of the Battle for Verdun, for example, historian, A. J. P. Taylor wrote, "Verdun was the most senseless episode in a war not distinguished for sense anywhere. Both sides at Verdun fought literally for the sake of fighting. There was no prize to be gained or lost, only men to be killed and glory to be won." A. J. P. Taylor, *A History of the First World War*, pp. 74–75, 76–77.
44. For brief details refer to A. W. Palmer, *A Dictionary of Modern History 1789–1945*, p. 170.
45. A. J. P. Taylor, *A History of the First World War*, pp. 109, 110, 113–14.
46. 'Abdu'l-Bahá, *Tablets of the Divine Plan*, ¶7.14.
47. Ibid., ¶8.20-21.
48. For a detailed treatment of the Tablets of the Divine Plan and their contents refer to Janet A. Khan, *Call to Apostleship: Reflections on the Tablets of the Divine Plan* (Wilmette: Bahá'í Publishing, 2016).

49. 'Abdu'l-Bahá, *Tablets of the Divine Plan,* ¶14.10.
50. Ibid., ¶11.14.
51. Ibid., ¶10.10.
52. See, for example, Abdu'l-Bahá, *Tablets of the Divine Plan,* ¶14.6 and ¶14.9.
53. 'Abdu'l-Bahá, *Tablets of the Divine Plan,* ¶12.5.
54. Ibid., ¶6.11, ¶6.4, and ¶6.7.
55. Ibid., ¶3.3.
56. Ibid., ¶1.3.

6 / Engaging in the Discourse on Universal Peace

1. "Iran and the First World War." http://www.iranreview.org. Copyright © 2007–2019 *Iran Review.* Atabaki, Touraj: Persia/Iran, in: 1914-1918-online. *International Encyclopedia of the First World War,* edited by Ute Daniel, Peter Gatrell, Oliver Janz, Heather Jones, Jennifer Keene, Alan Kramer, and Bill Nasson, issued by Freie Universität Berlin, Berlin May 2, 2016. DOI: 10.15463/ie1418.10899.
2. Ibid. DOI: 10.15463/ie1418.10899.
3. Djavadi, reported in *Iran and The Great War.* http://en.radiofarda.com. November 13, 2018.
4. Touraj: "Persia/Iran," in: 1914-1918-online. *International Encyclopedia of the First World War,* edited by Ute Daniel, Peter Gatrell, Oliver Janz, Heather Jones, Jennifer Keene, Alan Kramer, and Bill Nasson, issued by Freie Universität Berlin, Berlin. May 2, 2016. DOI: 10.15463/ie1418.10899.
5. Ibid.
6. "Qajar Dynasty." *Encyclopedia of the Modern Middle East and North Africa.* http://www.Encyclopedia.com. January 21, 2019 https://www.encyclopedia.com.
7. 1899: The principal delegate was Mírzá Riḍá Khán, Arfa'-al-Dawla (1846–1937), also known as Prince Riḍá Arfa'. Riḍá served as a Russian interpreter for Náṣiri'd-Dín Sháh during his journey across the Caucasus on the way to Europe in 1873 and subsequently in 1889. The shah expressed satisfaction with his services, and as a result Riḍá was appointed as third secretary at the Persian consulate in Tiflis. In 1895, he was named Persian minister to the Russian court at St. Petersburg and, in 1900, ambassador to the Ottoman court, a post that he held for ten years. In the same year he represented Persia at the peace conference in The Hague. http://www.iranicaonline.org/articles/danes-pen-name-of-moin-al-wezara-mirza-reza-khan-arfa-arfa-al-dawla-ca.

The second member of the delegation was Mírzá Samad Khán Momtas-as-Saltaneh, (1869–1955) an Iranian diplomat of the Qajar and Pahlavi dynasty era. In 1883, he was secretary of the legation in Paris. He later served as embassy counselor in St. Petersburg and participated in Náṣiri'd-Dín Sháh and then Moẓaffar'ed-Dín S͟háh's travels to Europe. He was minister of Persia in Belgium and the Netherlands before being appointed Extraordinary and Plenipotentiary Minister in Paris in April 1905. He served briefly as Prime Minister of Iran from 2 to 20 August 1918. In March 1921, he was elevated to the rank of Prince by Aḥmad S͟háh. http://enacademic.com/dic.nsf/enwiki/7779902.

8. There were three delegates to the 1907 Peace Conference at The Hague. The head of delegation was Mírzá Samad K͟hán Momtas-as-Saltaneh, (1869–1955), Envoy Extraordinary and Minister Plenipotentiary at Paris, who had also been appointed a member of the Permanent Court of Arbitration. The other two members were Mírzá Aḥmad K͟hán Sadig-ul-Mulkh, the Envoy Extraordinary and Minister Plenipotentiary at The Hague; and Mr. M. Hennebicq, the Legal adviser to the Minister of Foreign Affairs at Tehran, who served as the technical delegate. "Text of the Final Act," *The American Journal of International Law*, vol. 2, no. ½, Supplement: Official Documents (Jan.–Apr., 1908): 18. https://www.jstor.org/stable/2212498.

9. Betsy Baker, *Hague Peace Conferences 1899–1907*, Oxford Open Law, Oxford Public International law. http://opil.ouplaw.com/view/10.1093/law:epil/9780199231690/law-9780199231690-e305.

10. Mírzá Aḥmad K͟hán-i-Yazdání. The original short narrative is in Persian, and titled *S͟harḥ-i-Nuzúl-i-Lawḥ-i-Ṣulḥ-i-Láháy* (*The Account of the Revelation of the Peace Tablet to The Hague*). This narrative was sent by its author to Shoghi Effendi, who much appreciated its receipt, on 1 Bahá 94 B.E. The document was provided to the authors by the Research Department of the Universal House of Justice. June 13, 2018.

11. Oliver Bast, "Les « buts de guerre » de la Perse neutre pendant la Première Guerre mondiale" in *Relations internationales* 160 (1): 95 January 2015 with DOI: 10.3917/ri.160.0095.

12. See "In memoriam," *The Bahá'í World*, volume XIV, pp. 351–53.

13. "Chronology of Iranian History, Part 2." http://www.iranicaonline.org/pages/chronology-2.

14. "Anglos-Persian Agreement of 1919." http://www.iranicaonline.org/articles/anglo-persian-agreement-1919.

15. Detailed historical treatments of these subjects are found in such works as Shoghi Effendi, *God Passes By*, pp. 271–278 and pp. 326–337; Adib Taherzadeh, *The Revelation of Bahá'u'lláh*, volume 2, chapter 15 and Adib Taherzadeh, *The Revelation of Bahá'u'lláh*, volume 3, chapters 6–9; Peter J. Khan, *The Promised Day is Come, Study Guide* (Wilmette: Bahá'í Publishing Trust, 1967).

16. Soli Shahvar, *The Forgotten Schools, The Bahá'ís and Modern Education in Iran, 1899–1934*, pp. 4–6.

17. Ibid.

18. *Century of Light*, document prepared at the request of the Universal House of Justice, paragraphs 10.2–10.6.

19. See "In memoriam" *The Bahá'í World*, vol. XVII, pp. 438–40.

20. The newspaper article has not yet been located. See Appendix for a copy of the version of the Central Organization for a Durable Peace's manifesto and minimum-program as published in Doty, *The Central Organisation for A Durable Peace (1915–1919), Its History, Work and Ideas.*

21. See "In memoriam" *The Bahá'í World*, vol. XVII, pp. 438–40. The title of the Women's Magazine was Tará'niy-i-Umíd (Song of Hope), and the title of the Youth Magazine was Áhang-i Badí'.

22. Mírzá Aḥmad Khán-i-Yazdání. The original short narrative is in Persian, and titled *Sharḥ-i-Nuzúl-i-Lawḥ-i-ṣulḥ-i-Láháy (The Account of the Revelation of the Peace Tablet to The Hague).* This narrative was sent by its author to Shoghi Effendi, who much appreciated its receipt, on 1 Bahá 94 B.E. Document provided by the Research Department of the Universal House of Justice, June 13, 2018.

23. Ebn Aṣdaq, Mírzá Alí-Muḥammad (b. Mašhad 1850; d. Tehran, 1928). See entry in *Encyclopaedia Iranica*, volume 7.

24. Ibrahim Piruzbakht. For details, see *The Bahá'í World*, vol. VII, pp. 545–47.

25. See entry in *Encyclopaedia Iranica*, volume 7. http://www.iranicaonline.org/.

26. For details see *The Bahá'í World*, vol. VII, pp. 545–47.

27. Mírzá Aḥmad Khán-i-Yazdání. The original short narrative is in Persian, and titled *Sharḥ-i-Nuzúl-i-Lawḥ-i-Ṣulḥ-i-Láháy (The Account of the Revelation of the Peace Tablet to The Hague).* This narrative was sent by its author to Shoghi Effendi, who much appreciated its receipt, on 1 Bahá 94 B.E. Document provided by the Research Department of the Universal House of Justice, June 13, 2018.

28. This Tablet was written in Persian. Its English translation appears as item 1 in Appendix 2. See also https://www.bahai.org/library/authoritative-texts/abdul-baha/tablets-hague-abdul-baha/2#381373700.

29. Cited in *Star of the West*, vol. 11, no. 8 (August 1, 1920): 123. The Archives at the Bahá'í World Center does not hold any correspondence that led to the revelation of the Tablet dated December 17, 1919.

30. Mírzá Aḥmad Khán-i-Yazdání. The original short narrative is in Persian, and titled *Sharḥ-i-Nuzúl-i-Lawḥ-i-Ṣulḥ-i-Láháy (The Account of the Revelation of the Peace Tablet to The Hague).* This narrative was sent by its author to Shoghi Effendi, who much appreciated its receipt, on 1 Bahá 94 B.E. Document provided by the Research Department of the Universal House of Justice, June 13, 2018.

31. Ibid.

32. Information gleaned from Shoghangiz Yazdani-Javid, *Ahmad Yazdani, The Messenger of 'Abdu'l-Bahá's Teachings of Peace to The Hague, Holland.*

33. Mírzá Aḥmad Khán-i-Yazdání. The original short narrative is in Persian, and titled *Sharḥ-i-Nuzúl-i-Lawḥ-i-Ṣulḥ-i-Láháy* (*The Account of the Revelation of the Peace Tablet to The Hague*). This narrative was sent by its author to Shoghi Effendi, who much appreciated its receipt, on 1 Bahá 94 B.E. Document provided by the Research Department of the Universal House of Justice, 13 June 2018.

34. Mrs. A. J. Dyserinck. Research Department memorandum, June 13, 2018. As a delegate of one of the Dutch societies, *Bond ter Behartiging van de Belangen' van het Kind*, she participated in the International Congress of Women held at The Hague in April 1915. See details, http://www.ub.gu.se/kvinndata/portaler/fred/samarbete/pdf/congores_varouwen.pdf.

35. Hendrik Coenraad Dresselhuys (1870–1926) studied law, served as a judge, and was elected to the Dutch Parliament in 1916. From 1914 to 1919, he was chairman of the Dutch Anti-War Council (NAO) and was involved in setting up the Central Organization for a Durable Peace in 1915 and served as the president of its Executive Committee. After the war, he was convinced of the ability of the League of Nations to prevent a future world conflict. He passed away in 1926. In 1931, a monument was erected at the Carnegienlaan in The Hague in his honor. This monument was the work of Arend Willem Maurits Odé (1865–1955), professor of modeling and sculpture at the then Technical University of Delft. https://translate.google.com.au/translate?hl=en&sl=nl&u=https://nl.wikipedia.org/wiki/Hendrik_Coenraad_Dresselhuijs&prev=search

36. Mírzá Aḥmad Khán-i-Yazdání. The original short narrative is in Persian, and titled *Sharḥ-i-Nuzúl-i-Lawḥ-i-Ṣulḥ-i-Láháy* (*The Account of the Revelation of the Peace Tablet to The Hague*).

37. Ibid.

38. The Tablet dated December 17 and the Tablet addressed to the people of the world appear in Appendix 2. The Tablets are also published on https://www.bahai.org/library/authoritative-texts/abdul-baha/tablets-hague-abdul-baha/.

39. See paragraphs 1 and 4 of 'Abdu'l-Bahá's letter of December 17, 1919, item 1, Appendix 2.

40. The letter dated June 12, 1920, written in French by H. C. Dresselhuys to 'Abdu'l-Bahá, is held in the Archives at the Bahá'í World Center.

41. Mírzá Aḥmad Khán-i-Yazdání. The original short narrative is in Persian and titled *Sharḥ-i-Nuzúl-i-Lawḥ-i-Ṣulḥ-i-Láháy* (*The Account of the Revelation of the Peace Tablet to The Hague*).

42. To date, Yazdání's letter of June 14, 1920 has not been identified.

43. Reference to the First and Second Peace Conferences held at The Hague in 1899 and 1907.

44. 'Abdu'l-Bahá, *Selections from the Writings of 'Abdu'l-Bahá*, no. 228. The complete Tablet is published in this volume.

45. 'Abdu'l-Bahá's Second Tablet to The Hague, appears as item 2 in Appendix 2. Paragraphs cited 2–3. The Tablet is also published on https://www.bahai.org/library/authoritative-texts/abdul-baha/tablets-hague-abdul-baha/.
46. Mírzá Aḥmad Khán-i-Yazdání. The original short narrative is in Persian, and titled *Sharḥ-i-Nuzúl-i-Lawḥ-i-Ṣulḥ-i-Láháy* (*The Account of the Revelation of the Peace Tablet to The Hague*).
47. Information gleaned from Shoghangiz Yazdani-Javid, *AhmadYazdani, The Messenger of 'Abdu'l-Bahá's Teachings of Peace to The Hague, Holland.*

7 / Analysis of the Tablets to The Hague

1. The Universal House of Justice, in paragraph 2 of its letter dated January 18, 2019 to the Bahá'ís of the World, refers to the Paris Conference as the first historical moment "in the last one hundred years when its seemed as if the human race was reaching for real, lasting peace, albeit always falling short because of weaknesses it could not overcome."
2. Ronald N. Stromberg, "The Idea of Collective" *Journal of the History of Ideas*, vol. 17, no. 2 (April 1956): 250–63, 250. https://www.jstor.org/stable/2707745.
3. Ibid.
4. Charles Townshend, "The League of Nations and the United Nations," February 17, 2011. http://www.bbc.co.uk. February 25, 2019.
5. *Century of Light*, ¶3.39.
6. Kaiser, "Treaty of Versailles," *The Reader's Companion to Military History*. Edited by Robert Cowley and Geoffrey Parker. https://www.history.com/topics/world-war-i/treaty of Versailles-1. February 26, 2019. For additional details, see also https://www.britannica.com/topic/League-of-Nations. February 24, 2019.
7. The final text of the Covenant of the League of Nations was adopted on April 28, 1919 by the unanimous decision of the conference. The Covenant was a short and concise document of twenty-six articles. The first seven articles established the constitutional basis of the new system. They defined the League's original members; created the directing organs of the League—namely, an Assembly composed of representatives of all members and a Council initially composed of representatives of the United States, Great Britain, France, Italy and Japan as permanent members, with four others elected by the Assembly—created a permanent Secretariat, provided for the expenses of the League, and named Geneva as its headquarters. Articles 8 and 9 dealt with armaments, and a permanent commission was provided to advise the Council on all military, naval, and air questions.

Articles 10–17 embodied the central and basic idea of the League: collective security, together with the various procedures for peaceful settlement of disputes—arbitration, legal procedure, or action by the Council or the Assembly. These provisions included the establishment of a permanent international court. Articles 18–22 set out provisions pertaining to transparency and open diplomacy, preserved the Monroe Doctrine, and established the mandate system. Articles 23 and 24 concerned worldwide economic and social cooperation under the authority of the League. Members agreed to work together on such matters as transport and communications, commercial relations, health, supervision of the international arms trade, and bringing existing international agencies, such as the Universal Postal Union, under the direction of the League. League Members also agreed to set up an International Labour Organization. Article 25 promised support for the Red Cross. And Article 26 defined the procedure for amending the Covenant. https://www.britannica.com/topic/League-of-Nations. February 24, 2019.

8. Charles Townshend, "The League of Nations and the United Nations." February 17, 2011. http://www.bbc.co.uk. February 25, 2019.
9. For details, see https://www.britannica.com/topic/League-of-Nations. February 24, 2019.
10. Ibid.
11. Ibid.
12. Ibid.
13. Firuz Kazemzadeh, *Universal and Lasting Peace, Commentary on 'Abdu'l-Bahá's Tablet to the Hague,* pp. 7–8.
14. *Century of Light,* para. 3.41.
15. 'Abdu'l-Bahá, *Selections from the Writings of 'Abdu'l-Bahá,* no. 227.31.
16. Bahá'u'lláh, *The Tabernacle of Unity,* p. 23.
17. Appendix 2, item 1. https://www.bahai.org/library/authoritative-texts/abdul-baha/tablets-hague-abdul-baha/2#981582315
18. Appendix 2, item 2. https://www.bahai.org/library/authoritative-texts/abdul-baha/tablets-hague-abdul-baha/2#981582315
19. Circa 1870.
20. 'Abdu'l-Bahá, *Selections from the Writings of 'Abdu'l-Bahá,* no. 227.3.
21. 'Abdu'l-Bahá, Appendix 2, item 1.
22. Bahá'u'lláh, *Gleanings from the Writings of Bahá'u'lláh,* no. 120.1.
23. 'Abdu'l-Bahá, Appendix 2, item 1.
24. Ibid.
25. 'Abdu'l-Bahá, *Selections from the Writings of 'Abdu'l-Bahá,* no. 201.2.
26. Ibid.
27. *Century of Light,* ¶11.22.
28. 'Abdu'l-Bahá, Appendix 2, item 1.
29. Ibid.
30. Ibid.
31. 'Abdu'l-Bahá, *Selections from the Writings of 'Abdu'l-Bahá,* no. 227.21.

32. Ibid.
33. Ibid.
34. Ibid.
35. Ibid.
36. Ibid.
37. Ibid.
38. Shoghi Effendi, *Citadel of Faith: Messages to America 1947–1957,* p. 36.
39. For information on this subject refer to Moojan Momen, Ed. *The Bábí and Bahá'í Religions, 1844–1944, Some Contemporary Western Accounts,* footnote on pp. 324–25.
40. 'Abdu'l-Bahá, Appendix 2, item 1.
41. Ibid.
42. Ibid.
43. For Bahá'ís the "Word of God" refers to the Writings revealed by Bahá'u'lláh and the prophet founders of major religions. Perhaps it may be understood most broadly as spiritual reality and its power to uplift the human spirit and transform the social order. 'Abdu'l-Bahá explains: "the Word of God is sanctified above all these conditions and exalted beyond every law, constraint, or limitation that may exist in the contingent world." See 'Abdu'l-Bahá, *Some Answered Questions,* p. 173.
44. 'Abdu'l-Bahá, Appendix 2, item 1.
45. 'Abdu'l-Bahá, Appendix 2, item 1(a).
46. Ibid.
47. Ibid.
48. Ibid.
49. Ibid.
50. 'Abdul-Bahá, Appendix 2, item 2.
51. Ibid.
52. Ibid.
53. Ibid.
54. Ibid.
55. Ibid.
56. Ibid.
57. Ibid.
58. Ibid.

8 / The Emergence of Peace

1. The Universal House of Justice, letter to the Bahá'ís of the World, January 18, 2019, paragraph 1.
2. Bahá'u'lláh, cited in Shoghi Effendi, extract from a letter dated March 11, 1936, *The World Order of Bahá'u'lláh,* p. 202.

3. See, for example, Shoghi Effendi, *The World Order of Bahá'u'lláh*, William S. Hatcher & J. Douglas Martin, *The Bahá'í Faith: The Emerging Global Religion*, pp. 143–44.
4. For a detailed discussion of the United Nations refer to http://www.un.org.
5. *Charter of the United Nations*, Preamble. http://www.un.org/en/charter-united-nations.
6. *Charter of the United Nations*, Chapter VI. http://www.un.org.
7. *Charter of the United Nations*, Chapter VII. http://www.un.org. See also Jacques Fomerand, Cecelia M. Lynch, Karen Mingst, "United Nations." https://www.britannica.com.
8. For details refer to Jacques Fomerand, Cecelia M. Lynch, Karen Mingst, "United Nations." https://www.britannica.com.
9. *Charter of the United Nations*, Chapter X, Article 68. http://www.un.org.
10. "UN Universal Declaration of Human Rights." http://www.humanrights.com.
11. *Charter of the United Nations*, Chapter XIV. http://www.un.org. See also Jacques Fomerand, Cecelia M. Lynch, Karen Mingst, "United Nations," https://www.britannica.com.
12. Jacques Fomerand, Cecelia M. Lynch, Karen Mingst, "United Nations." https://www.britannica.com.
13. Ibid.
14. Ibid.
15. The Universal House of Justice, *Century of Light*, para. 6.20.
16. Letter dated April 19, 2001, written on behalf of the Universal House of Justice to an individual, paragraph 6.
17. The Universal House of Justice, letter dated January 18, 2019 to the Bahá'ís of the World.
18. The Universal House of Justice, message of Riḍván 158 B.E. (2001) to the Bahá'ís of the World.
19. The Universal House of Justice, message of Riḍván 153 B.E. (1996) to the Bahá'ís of the World.
20. The Global Financial Crisis of 1997–98.
21. The Universal House of Justice, message of Riḍván 155 B.E. (1998) to the Bahá'ís of the World.
22. The Universal House of Justice, message of Riḍván 157 B.E. (2000) to the Bahá'ís of the World.
23. The Universal House of Justice, letter dated January 18, 2019 to the Bahá'ís of the World.
24. Ibid.
25. Shoghi Effendi, *Citadel of Faith: Messages to America, 1947–1957*, p. 33.
26. The Universal House of Justice, letter dated January 18, 2019 to the Bahá'ís of the World.

27. Ibid.
28. 'Abdu'l-Bahá, *The Secret of Divine Civilization*, ¶8–9.
29. The Universal House of Justice, *Century of Light* (Haifa: Bahá'í World Centre, 2001), para. 11.22. In 1985, the Universal House of Justice offered the global Bahá'í community as a "model for study that could reinforce hope in the possibility of uniting the human race." Since then, that community has been "patiently refining that model and working with others around them to build up and broaden a system of social organization" based on Bahá'u'lláh's teachings (The Universal House of Justice, letter dated January 18, 2019 to the Bahá'ís of the World). Bahá'ís invite others to join in this learning process with them and also seek to share the fruits of their experience: "[T]the capacity created in the Bahá'í community over successive global Plans renders it increasingly able to lend assistance in the manifold and diverse dimensions of civilization building, opening to it new frontiers of learning" (The Universal House of Justice, Riḍván 2010 message to the Bahá'ís of the World).
30. 'Abdu'l-Bahá, *Selections from the Writings of 'Abdu'l-Bahá*, ¶15.6.
31. The Universal House of Justice, message of Riḍván 173 B.E. (2016) to the Bahá'ís of the World.

Appendix 1
1. "The Oneness of the Reality of Humankind." https://centenary.bahai.us/talk/oneness-reality-humankind.

Appendix 2
1. "Tablets to The Hague." https://www.bahai.org/library/authoritative-texts/abdul-baha/tablets-hague-abdul-baha/4#586879981.
2. Ibid.
3. Ibid.

Bibliography

Writings of Bahá'u'lláh

Epistle to the Son of the Wolf. Wilmette, IL: Bahá'í Publishing Trust, 1988.

Gleanings from the Writings of Bahá'u'lláh. Translated by Shoghi Effendi. New ed. Wilmette, IL: Bahá'í Publishing, 2005.

Tablets of Bahá'u'lláh Revealed after the Kitáb-i-Aqdas. Compiled by the Research Department of the Universal House of Justice and translated by Habib Taherzadeh with the assistance of a Committee at the Bahá'í World Center. Wilmette, IL: Bahá'í Publishing Trust, 1988.

The Kitáb-i-Aqdas: The Most Holy Book. Wilmette, IL: Bahá'í Publishing Trust, 1993.

The Summons of the Lord of Hosts: Tablets of Bahá'u'lláh. Wilmette, IL: Bahá'í Publishing, 2006.

The Tabernacle of Unity. Haifa: Bahá'í World Center, 2006.

Writings of 'Abdu'l-Bahá

'Abdu'l-Bahá in Canada. Forest: National Spiritual Assembly of Canada, 1962.

Paris Talks: Addresses Given by 'Abdu'l-Bahá in 1911. Wilmette, IL: Bahá'í Publishing, 2011.

Selections from the Writings of 'Abdu'l-Bahá. Wilmette, IL: Bahá'í Publishing, 2010.

Tablets of the Divine Plan. Wilmette, IL: Bahá'í Publishing Trust, 1993.

Promulgation of Universal Peace: Talks Delivered by 'Abdu'l-Bahá During His Visit to the United States and Canada in 1912. Wilmette, IL: Bahá'í Publishing, 2012.

The Secret of Divine Civilization. Translated from the Persian by Marzieh Gail in consultation with Ali-Kuli Khan. Wilmette, IL: Bahá'í Publishing, 2007.

Bibliography

Writings of Shoghi Effendi

Citadel of Faith: Messages to America, 1947–1957. Wilmette: Bahá'í Publishing Trust, 1965. 2014 printing.

God Passes By. Wilmette: Bahá'í Publishing Trust, 1965. Revised edition 1974. Ninth printing 2018.

Messages to the Bahá'í World, 1950–1957. Wilmette, IL: Bahá'í Publishing Trust, 1971.

"The Faith of Bahá'u'lláh, A World Religion." *World Order.* Vol. XIII, no. 7. October 1947.

The Proclamation of Bahá'u'lláh. Haifa: Bahá'í World Center, 1967.

The Promised Day is Come. Wilmette, IL: Bahá'í Publishing Trust, 1993.

The World Order of Bahá'u'lláh: Selected Letters. New ed. Wilmette, IL: Bahá'í Publishing Trust, 1991.

This Decisive Hour: Message from Shoghi Effendi to the North American Bahá'ís, 1932–1946. Wilmette, IL: Bahá'í Publishing Trust, 2002.

Writings of the Universal House of Justice

Message of Riḍván to the Bahá'ís of the World, 153 B.E. (1996).

Message of Riḍván to the Bahá'ís of the World, 155 B.E. (1998).

Message of Riḍván to the Bahá'ís of the World, 157 B.E. (2000).

Message of Riḍván to the Bahá'ís of the World, 168 B.E. (2011).

Letter dated March 2, 2013 to the Bahá'ís of Iran.

Message of Riḍván, 173 B.E. (2016) to the Bahá'ís of the World.

Letter dated January 18, 2019 to the Bahá'ís of the World.

Other Works

Andrews, Fannie Fern. "Preparedness and America's International Program." *The Annals of the American Academy of Political and Social Science,* vol. 66, (July 1916). https://www.jstor.org/stable/1013420. Accessed December 19, 2018.

Atabaki, Touraj. "Persia/Iran." *International Encyclopedia of the First World War,* edited by Ute Daniel, Peter Gatrell, Oliver Janz, Heather Jones, Jennifer Keene, Alan Kramer, and Bill Nasson. issued by Freie Universität Berlin, Berlin. May 2, 2016. DOI: 10.15463/ie1418.10899.

Bahá'í International Community. *Who is Writing the Future?* New York: Bahá'í International Community, 1999.

Baker, Betsy. *Hague Peace Conferences 1899 1907.* Oxford Open Law, Oxford Public International law. http://opil.ouplaw.com/view/10.1093/law:epil/9780199231690/law-9780199231690-e305.

Balyuzi, H.M. *'Abdu'l-Bahá: The Centre of the Covenant.* Oxford: George Ronald, 1987.

Bibliography

Bast, Oliver. "Les [buts de guerre] de la Perse neutre pendant la Première Guerre mondiale." *Relations internationales* 160, no. 1 (January 2015): 95. DOI: 10.3917/ri.160.0095.

Bellah, Robert N. *Religion in Human Evolution: From the Paleolithic to the Axial Age.* Cambridge, MA: The Belknap Press of Harvard University Press, 2011.

Blom, Phillip. *The Vertigo Years: Europe, 1900–1914.* (New York: Basic Books, 2008).

Blomfield, Lady. *The Chosen Highway* Wilmette, IL: Bahá'í Publishing Trust, n.d.

Century of Light. Document commissioned by the Universal House of Justice. Bahá'í World Center, 2002.

Chatfield, Charles and van den Dungen, Peter (eds.): *Peace Movements and Political Cultures.* Knoxville University of Tennessee Press, 1988.

Cohen, Laurie R. "Fighting for Peace Amid Paralyzed Popular Opinion: Bertha von Suttner's and Rosa Mayreder's Pacifist-Feminist Insights on Gender, War and Peace," in Bruna Bianchi, Geraldine Ludbrook, eds. *Living War, Thinking Peace (1914–1924): Women's Experiences, Feminist Thought, and International Relations.* Newcastle upon Tyne, UK: Cambridge Scholars Publishing, 2016.

Cooper, Sandi. Patriotic Pacifism. Waging War on War in Europe, 1815–1914. New York: Oxford University Press, 1991.

Dickinson, G. Lowes. *Problems of the International Settlement.* New York: The Macmillan Company, 1919.

Doty, Madeline Z. *The Central Organisation for A Durable Peace (1915–1919), Its History, Work and Ideas.* Université de Genève, Institut Universitaire de Hautes Études Internationales: 1945.

Du Bois, W. E. B. *The Souls of Black Folk.* New York: Penguin, 1903.

Egea, Amín. *The Apostle of Peace, A Survey of References to 'Abdu'l-Bahá in the Western Press, 1871–1921.* Volume 1: 1871–1912. Oxford: George Ronald, 2017.

Eisenstadt, S. N. "The Axial Age Breakthroughs—Their Characteristics and Origins." Eisenstadt, S. N., ed., *The Origins and Diversity of the Axial Age* Albany: SUNY Press, 1986.

Ferguson, Niall. *The War of the World: History's Age of Hatred.* London: Penguin Books, 2007.

Fomerand, Jacques, Cecelia M. Lynch, and Karen Mingst. "United Nations." https://www.britannica.com.

Hatcher, William S. and J. Douglas Martin. *The Bahá'í Faith: The Emerging Global Religion.* Wilmette: Bahá'í Publishing, 2002.

Hayashi, Nobuo. *The Role and Importance of the Hague Conferences: A Historical Perspective.* UNIDIR 2017.

Held, D. *Democracy and the Global Order: From the Modern State to Global Governance.* Cambridge: Polity Press, 1995.

Bibliography

Higgins, A Pearce. *The Hague Peace Conferences, and other International Conferences Concerning the Laws and Usages of War.* Cambridge: University Press, 1909.

Hobsbawm, Eric. "Barbarism: A User's Guide." *On History.* New York: The New Press, 1997.

———. *The Age of Empire: 1875–1914.* New York: Vintage Books, 1989.

Josephson, Harold et al (eds.): *Biographical Dictionary of Modern Peace Leaders.* Westport, CT: Greenwood Press, 1985.

Kaiser, David. "Treaty of Versailles." *The Reader's Companion to Military History.* Edited by Robert Cowley and Geoffrey Parker. Boston: Houghton Mifflin Harcourt Publishing Company, 1996. https://www.history.com/topics/world-war-i/treaty of Versailles-1. Accessed February 26, 2019.

Kazemzadeh, Firuz. *Universal and Lasting Peace: Commentary on 'Abdu'l-Bahá's Tablet to the Hague.* Wilmette: Bahá'í Publishing Trust, 1970.

Khan, Janet A. *Call to Apostleship: Reflections on the Tablets of the Divine Plan.* Wilmette: Bahá'í Publishing, 2016.

Kissinger, Henry. *World Order.* New York: Penguin Press, 2014.

Krisch, N. *Beyond Constitutionalism: The Pluralist Structure of Postnational Law.* Oxford: Oxford University Press, 2010.

Lauren, Paul Gordon. *Power and Prejudice: The Politics and Diplomacy of Racial Discrimination.* New York, Routledge; 2 edition 1996.

Lukacs, John. *Remembered Past: A Reader.* Wilmington, DE: ISI Books, 2005.

Mahmoudi, Hoda. "Human Knowledge and the Advancement of Society." *The Journal of Bahá'í Studies.* Vol. 22, nos. 1–4. Ottawa: 2012.

Mazlish, B. and A. Iriye, eds. *The Global History Reader.* Abingdon: Routledge, 2005.

McEvedy, Colin. *The Century World History Factfinder.* London: Century Publishing, 1984.

Momen, Moojan, ed. *The Bábí and Bahá'í Religions, 1844–1944: Some Contemporary Western Accounts.* Oxford: George Ronald, 1981.

Nicolson, Juliet. *The Perfect Summer: England 1911, Just Before the Storm.* New York: Grove Press, 2006.

Nussbaum, M. *For Love of Country: Debating the Limits of Patriotism.* Boston, MA: Beacon Press, 1996.

Palmer, A. W. *A Dictionary of Modern History 1789–1945.* Baltimore, MD: Penguin Books, 1964.

Patterson, David S. "Pacifism." *International Encyclopedia of the First World War.* edited by Ute Daniel, Peter Gatrell, Oliver Janz, Heather Jones, Jennifer Keene, Alan Kramer, and Bill Nasson. Issued by Freie Universität Berlin. October 5, 2014. DOI: 10.15463/ie1418.10125.

"Qajar Dynasty." *Encyclopedia of the Modern Middle East and North Africa.* January 21, 2019. https://www.encyclopedia.com.

Bibliography

Shahvar, Soli. *The Forgotten Schools, The Baha'is and Modern Education in Iran, 1899–1934*. London: Tauris Academic Studies, 2009.

Star of the West.

Strachan, Hew. *The First World War*. London: Simon & Schuster, 2014.

Stromberg, Ronald N. "The Idea of Collective." *Journal of the History of Ideas.* Vol. 17, no. 2 (April 1956): 250–263, 250. https://www.jstor.org/stable/2707745.

Taylor, A. J. P. Cited in "Western Europe." http://www.historyhome.co.uk/europe/causeww1.htm. August 26, 2019.

Taherzadeh, Adib. *The Revelation of Bahá'u'lláh*. Volumes 2 and 3. Oxford: George Ronald, 1992 and 1996.

Tryon, James L. "The Hague Conferences." *The Yale Law Journal.* Vol. 20, no. 6 (April 1911). https://www.jstor.org/stable/784505. Accessed October 7, 2018.

Tuchman, Barbara. *The Proud Tower: A Portrait of the World Before the War, 1890–1914*. New York: Random House Trade Paperbacks, 2014.

Various articles. http://www.iranicaonline.org.

Wells, H. G. *A Short History of the World*. Mitcham, Victoria: Penguin Books, Pty., Ltd., 1960.

Williamson, Samuel R., Jr. "The Way to War." https://encyclopedia.1914-1918-online.net/article/the_way_to_war. August 26, 2019.

Wolke, Robert L. "Marie Curie's Doctoral Thesis: Prelude to a Nobel Prize." *Journal of Chemical Education.* Volume 65, no. 7 (July 1988): 561–73.

Wright, Esmond. *History of the World: the Last Five Hundred Years*. London: Newnes Books, 1984.

Yazdání, Aḥmad. *Sharḥ-i-Nuzúl-i-Lawḥ-i-Ṣulḥ-i-Láháy* (*The Account of the Revelation of the Peace Tablet to The Hague*). No date. Excerpts from this document were attached to a memorandum dated June 13, 2018 prepared by the Research Department at the Bahá'í World Center, and shared with the authors with the permission of The Universal House of Justice.

Yazdani-Javid, Shoghangiz. *Ahmad Yazdani: The Messenger of 'Abdu'l-Baha's Teachings of Peace to The Hague, Holland*. Los Angeles, 2008. Translated from the Persian.

Zürn, Michael. *A Theory of Global Governance: Authority, Legitimacy, and Contestation*. Oxford: Oxford University Press, 2018.

Index

Index

B

Báb, the
    followers of, 9
    Herald of Bahá'u'lláh, 9
    Mírzá 'Alí-Muḥammad name of, 9
Bahá'í community
    mission a spiritual enterprise, 98
    task of as described by 'Abdu'l-Bahá, 135
    various backgrounds of members, 160
Bahá'í Faith
    global religion, 11
    lack of priesthood, 22
    message of, 7–8
    objective of, 3
    origins of, 12
    principal aim of, 7
    principles of pertaining to peace, 2
    religion of constant change, 99
    source of religious, moral, and social modernism in
        Iran, 109
Bahá'ís. *See* Bahá'í community.
Bahá'u'lláh
    Founder of the Bahá'í Faith, ix
    manifold principles of, 137
    Mírzá Ḥusayn-'Alí name of, 9
    passing of, 80
    Tablets to kings and rulers, 16, 92–93
Baroness Bertha von Suttner, 52–53

C

Central Organization for a Durable Peace at The Hague
    dissolution of, 75–77
    establishment of, 65–72
    first letter to 'Abdu'l-Bahá, 110
    work of, 4
collective security, 15–16, 148
Colonel Ibráhím Pírúzbakht, 112
compelling power of conscience, 142
Congress of Vienna, 32

Index

Index

I

Ibn-i-Aṣdaq
Imperial Age, 32
imperialism, 45
independent investigation of reality, 136
Industrial Age, 35
Iran

K

kings

L

Lake Mohonk Peace Conference, 2
League of Nations, 128–31
Lesser Peace, 27, 148

M

Manifestations of God
Messengers of God.

women
    equality with men, 25
    status of before World War I, 42–43
Women's International League for Peace and Freedom, 72–74
Word of God, 139
world, 3
world consciousness
    awareness of oneness of humanity, 148
    role of United Nations and, 153
World Order of Bahá'u'lláh, ix, 21
    world's equilibrium upset by, 20
World War I
    catastrophic impact of, ix
    end of, 5
    forces for change leading up to, 3
    outbreak predicted by 'Abdu'l-Bahá, 28
    protagonists of, 48–50
    situation in Iran during, 4
    state of the world prior to, 2
World War II, 39

Y

Young Turk Revolution, 81